DIESEL DAYS
Scotland

DIESEL DAYS

Scotland

Brian J. Dickson

Ian Allan PUBLISHING

Contents

Front cover:
In strong spring sunshine, re-engined NBL Type 2 No D6103 winds its way through the Monnessie Gorge, between Roy Bridge and Tulloch, at the head of the morning train from Mallaig to Glasgow on an April day in 1968.

Back cover, top:
With a spectacular back-drop of rhododendron bushes, English Electric Type 1 No D8115 heads an Ayr-Girvan goods through Maybole station in June 1968.

Back cover, lower:
Hurrying north with a train comprising four Mk 1 coaches, BRCW/Sulzer Type 2 No D5302 is seen near Stow on a Hawick-Edinburgh working on Wednesday 3 November 1965. *All the late Derek Cross, courtesy David Cross*

Half-title:
Tuesday 2 August 1966
Passing a Standard Class 4 2-6-0 with a train of empty coal wagons, BR/Sulzer Type 4 No D30 heads through Kilmarnock with the up 'Thames–Clyde Express'. Renumbered 45 029, the diesel would be withdrawn initially in January 1981, reinstated and withdrawn again in July 1987 to be transferred into Departmental stock as No 97 410, final withdrawal coming in August 1988. *Derek Cross*

Title page:
Wednesday 7 July 1965
English Electric Type 4 No D357 speeds past Dunbar towards Edinburgh on the down main line at the head of a Class 7 goods train. The unused remains of Dunbar locomotive shed can be seen in the background. The locomotive would be withdrawn from service in July 1983 as No 40 157. *Author*

First published 2005

ISBN 0 7110 3070 7

© Brian J. Dickson 2005

Published by Ian Allan Publishing

an imprint of Ian Allan Publishing Ltd, Hersham, Surrey KT12 4RG.
Printed in England by Ian Allan Printing Ltd, Hersham, Surrey KT12 4RG.

Code: 0501/B1

This book is dedicated to my wife, for her continued perseverance and patience.

Introduction

In December 1954, when the British Transport Commission published its plan for the 'Modernisation and Re-equipment of British Railways', the number of main-line diesels operating on British Railways was seven — the two LMS-designed Co-Cos (Nos 10000/1), the Fell 2-D-2 locomotive (No 10100), the three Southern Region 1Co-Co1s (Nos 10201-3) and the LMS-designed Bo-Bo (No 10800) built by the North British Locomotive Co (NBL). The prototype 'Deltic' did not arrive until the end of 1955.

Likewise, diesel shunting locomotives were relatively few. The LMS had invested in the 0-6-0 diesel-electric 300/350hp-engined type before World War 2, but there were only a few working around the country until 1953, when BR started to produce large numbers of its own 0-6-0 diesel-electric shunter closely modelled on the successful LMS type. The Modernisation Plan makes it clear that the elimination of shunting work by steam locomotives was to be achieved within 15 years — by 1970! Thus it was that, by the late 1950s, various types of diesel shunters were working from Scottish depots. These included the standard BR-built 350hp 0-6-0 diesel-electric (Class 08), Hunslet 0-6-0 diesel-mechanical (Class 05), Barclay 0-4-0 diesel-mechanical (Class 06) and North British Locomotive 0-4-0 diesel-hydraulic (unclassified) designs, which were to be seen working across the Region, shunting larger goods yards, small station yards and performing station pilot duties at many of the large city stations. As the Plan envisaged, they were rapidly replacing steam shunting locomotives, such that by 1960 virtually all shunting duties throughout the Region were being carried out by diesels.

In late 1952 the Railway Executive, in an effort to improve revenue from branch and cross-country services, had announced a programme for the introduction of diesel multiple-units (DMUs), and by December 1954 the first units had been delivered from Derby Works and were starting work on services in the West Riding of Yorkshire.

In locomotive terms the Modernisation Plan predicted the end of steam power by announcing that no new steam locomotives would be built after the end of the 1956 programme. Reasons cited were, in no particular order, the difficulty of attracting labour for the tasks of cleaning, firing and servicing, the greater cleanliness of trains and stations, the demands for reduction in air pollution, the growing shortage

Tuesday 10 September 1968
Early morning at Kershope Foot station, with BR/Sulzer Type 2 No D5072 about to depart with the 07.06 Edinburgh–Carlisle. The 34G (Finsbury Park) shedcode plate reveals that the locomotive is a long way from home. Latterly numbered 24 072, it would be withdrawn in October 1975. *Andrew Muckley*

of large coal suitable for steam locomotives and the need for better acceleration. Although the Plan also recognised the advantages of the steam locomotive, such as low first-build cost, simplicity, robustness and long life, it added that the end of the steam era was nigh.

Although electrification was the ultimate goal, diesel traction, particularly with electric transmission, was seen as the way forward, and an initial programme, the Pilot Scheme, was devised whereby 174 main-line diesel locomotives would be purchased from various manufacturers — 160 with electric transmission and 14 with hydraulic transmission specifically for the Western Region. These were to be in three power groups:

Type A	600-1,000hp
Type B	1,000-1,250hp
Type C	2,000hp and over

These three groups later became five:

Type 1	1,000hp or less
Type 2	1,000-1,500hp
Type 3	1,500-2,000hp
Type 4	2,000-3,000hp
Type 5	3,000hp and over

The initial orders fell into the groups shown in the table below.

The initial intention was that, as the various types of Pilot Scheme locomotives were delivered, they would undergo intensive evaluation trials. But the policy soon changed to one whereby these locomotives were put into revenue-earning service as quickly as possible. To hasten the demise of steam many manufacturing orders were increased before completion and testing of the initial orders. Hence such types as the NBL/MAN Type 2 (Class 21), although quickly recognised as having a troublesome engine, reached a final build total of 58 locomotives.

The numbering for these new diesel locomotives had been fixed in 1957, prior to their introduction, with the use of a four-digit number and a 'D' prefix. Diesel shunters built prior to 1957 that bore five-figure numbers were allocated a new number with a 'D' prefix. In September 1968, with the end of standard-gauge steam on British Railways, the use of the 'D' prefix was discontinued. In practice locomotives started to lose the 'D' prefix either when they went into workshops for overhaul or when individual depots started to paint out the 'D'. Either way, a large number of locomotives kept the 'D' prefix for many years after the 1968 decision. A number of photographs in this book show locomotives between September 1968 and 1972 still proudly bearing the 'D'. In 1972 the present Total Operations Processing System (TOPS) was introduced, locomotives being allocated a two-digit class number followed by an individual serial number; thus, for example, English Electric Type 1 (Class 20) No D8031 became 20 031.

The 'dieselisation' of traffic in Scotland started with passenger services on branch, inter-city and cross-country

Type	TOPS class	Builder	Engine power	Wheel arr	Transmission	Initial order	Delivered	Number series
1	15	Clayton *	800hp	Bo-Bo	Electric	10	1957>	D8200>
1	16	NBL	800hp	Bo-Bo	Electric	10	1958>	D8400>
1	20	English Electric	1,000hp	Bo-Bo	Electric	20	1957>	D8000>
2	21	NBL	1,000hp	Bo-Bo	Electric	10	1958>	D6100>
2	22	NBL	1,000hp	B-B	Hydraulic	6	1958>	D6300>
2	23	English Electric	1,100hp	Bo-Bo	Electric	10	1959>	D5900>
2	24	BR Derby	1,160hp	Bo-Bo	Electric	20	1958>	D5000>
2	26	BRCW	1,160hp	Bo-Bo	Electric	20	1958>	D5300>
2	28	Metropolitan-Vickers	1,200hp	Co-Bo	Electric	20	1958>	D5700>
2	30	Brush	1,250hp	A1A-A1A	Electric	20	1957>	D5500>
4	40	English Electric	2,000hp	1Co-Co1	Electric	10	1958>	D200>
4	41	NBL	2,000hp	A1A-A1A	Hydraulic	5	1957>	D600>
4	42	BR Swindon	2,000hp	B-B	Hydraulic	3	1958>	D800>
4	44	BR Derby	2,300hp	1Co-Co1	Electric	10	1959>	D1>

* construction sub-contracted to Yorkshire Engine Co

Monday 13 September 1965
Bathed in strong summer sunshine, a two-car Gloucester DMU waits to leave North Berwick as the 13.33 to Corstorphine.
R. F. Roberts

routes using DMUs and railbuses. Swindon-built six-car DMUs (later Class 126) were introduced in January 1957 on the intensive Edinburgh Waverley – Glasgow Queen Street service and were a great success. Throughout 1958 the suburban and branch services around Edinburgh saw the introduction of Gloucester RCW two-car DMUs (Class 100), working the services to Corstorphine, North Berwick, Musselburgh, Leith North, Peebles and Galashiels and, of course, the intensive service on the suburban Inner Circle and Outer Circle; these two-car units were also to be seen working Larbert, Polmont and Grangemouth services. Additionally, during 1958 Metro-Cammell-built two-car DMUs (Class 101) were being delivered to Scotland and could be seen working stopping services between Dundee and Glasgow and some Dundee–Edinburgh stopping trains; these units, based in Dundee, were also introduced on local services to Tayport, Leuchars Junction and St Andrews.

The British Transport Commission further thought that the introduction of four-wheel railbuses to sparsely populated branches and lines would further reduce costs and increase revenue. So, from the spring of 1959 these were tried with limited success on the Speyside line between Elgin and Aviemore and on the Dalmellington branch in Ayrshire. Similarly, the beautiful but sparsely populated Devon Valley line, between Stirling and Kinross, and the Crieff–Comrie branch also saw the use of railbuses from the spring of 1959.

In August 1959 the second batch of Swindon-built three- and six-car DMUs (Class 126) were delivered to the Glasgow area to work the services from St Enoch to Ayr, Girvan and Stranraer, as well as to Ardrossan and to Largs. By the summer of 1960 Swindon-built three-car DMUs (Class 120) were operating some services between Aberdeen and Inverness, the guard's compartments having been fitted with automatic tablet-exchange equipment to enable non-stop running on the single-track sections. Cravens-built two-car DMUs (Class 105) started to appear on the Scottish Region in the summer of 1959, working services to East Kilbride and on the Cathcart Circle in Glasgow; they were also seen working out of Aberdeen on the line to Ballater, and when steam was withdrawn from the isolated St Combs branch from Fraserburgh it was a Cravens two-car unit that took over and operated the service for many years. By 1960 Derby-built three-car units (Class 107) were being delivered to the Glasgow area, primarily for use on the South Side suburban services.

While the introduction of DMUs was proceeding the first batches of main-line diesel locomotives were appearing from the builders. In 1957, the first examples of the English Electric Type 1 were delivered, with further batches following rapidly. These quickly proved themselves to be reliable locomotives, and some of the earlier examples were allocated to Scottish depots such as Inverness and Kittybrewster in Aberdeen. These locomotives were to be seen regularly working pick-up goods trains on the Speyside lines and also the Peterhead/Fraserburgh–Aberdeen fish trains.

During 1958 the North British Locomotive Co began testing its MAN-engined Type 2 (Class 21) locomotives which, early in 1959, started to arrive in the Eastern Region's London area for suburban passenger duties. However, it quickly became apparent that major technical problems were being identified with their overall performance, and by the end of 1960 all had been reallocated to Scottish depots — initially Eastfield in Glasgow and Kittybrewster in Aberdeen — to be closer to the manufacturer for repairs. The Glasgow-based locomotives would soon be seen working over most of the Scottish Region, on passenger trains from Glasgow to Fort William and Mallaig, Glasgow to Oban and Glasgow to Dundee and Aberdeen, while the Aberdeen examples could be observed plodding their way around the Buchan branches to Peterhead and Fraserburgh and hauling passenger trains from Aberdeen to Elgin and Forres. In an attempt to improve reliability No D6123 was re-engined during 1963 with a Paxman unit. After satisfactory testing a further 19 locomotives were so treated, and the 20 re-engined locomotives re-designated as Class 29. Withdrawal of both classes started in 1968, the last being taken out of service in 1971.

By the middle of 1958 Derby Works had started to deliver the initial batch of its Pilot Scheme Type 2 (Class 24) locomotives. Powered by Sulzer engines, these very quickly became one of the most widely allocated and successful of the Pilot Scheme Type 2 designs. Further batches were built by the BR works at Derby, Crewe and Darlington, and 19 locomotives from these first batches were allocated to Inverness depot. These could be seen working both passenger and goods trains as far afield as Wick, Thurso, Kyle of Lochalsh and, in pairs, to Edinburgh with passenger workings from Inverness. This Type 2 was so successful that a more powerful variant (Class 25) was designed and introduced in 1961, being built at Darlington, Derby and the Beyer-Peacock works. Around 20 examples of this class were allocated to Eastfield depot in Glasgow during 1966.

Rivalling the BR Type 2 was the Birmingham Railway Carriage & Wagon Co (BRCW) Type 2 (later Class 26), being a further Sulzer-engined Pilot Scheme design introduced in 1958. The first 20 locomotives were delivered to Hornsey depot, but from 1960 these were reallocated to Scotland, primarily Haymarket in Edinburgh and Inverness, where they joined the remaining 27. These locomotives could be seen working singly or in pairs all over the Scottish Region, many surviving until the early 1990s. Again, because of their initial success, further orders were placed for a more powerful version (Class 27), introduced in 1961, the first 22 being allocated to Thornton and Eastfield in Glasgow.

Introduced in 1958, the English Electric Type 4 (Class 40) quickly became another of the successes of the Pilot Scheme, with repeat orders being placed before the first batch of locomotives had entered service. In 1960 seven were allocated to Haymarket, where they were joined in 1961 by a further batch of 12, and these were to be seen working passenger trains to Aberdeen and hauling named expresses such as the 'Queen of Scots' Pullman, 'Talisman' and 'North Briton' on the East Coast main line. English-based examples were to be seen working into Scotland on the West Coast main line, hauling such expresses as the 'Royal Scot', 'Mid-Day Scot' and 'Caledonian' into Glasgow Central. The class finally numbered 200 locomotives, most of which survived until the early 1980s.

Another successful Pilot Scheme Type 4, introduced in 1959, was the Sulzer-engined, Derby-built 'Peak' class (later designated Class 44). Later orders were for more powerful versions, introduced in 1960 (Class 45) and 1961 (Class 46), built at both Derby and Crewe, but were all part of the 'Peak' family. None was initially allocated to Scotland, but many were to be seen working passenger and goods trains over the old 'Sou'West' route between Glasgow and Carlisle, the 'Thames–Clyde Express' being a regular turn. Another regular duty was the 'Waverley' passenger working between London St Pancras and Edinburgh Waverley, which traversed the rugged Settle–Carlisle line and the Waverley route, the whole journey taking over nine hours to complete.

In 1961 British Railways started to take delivery of the most powerful of its early diesel locomotives with the arrival of the English Electric Type 5 (Class 55) 'Deltics'. Twenty-two of these had been ordered to replace steam traction working express passenger traffic on the East Coast main line, and eight were based at Haymarket. Along with their classmates based at King's Cross they were soon handling all the major express passenger trains on the route and earned their keep in this way for nearly 20 years until replaced by InterCity 125 High Speed Trains. They were reliable and successful, and, despite their high maintenance costs, proved themselves worthy successors to the steam locomotives they replaced. Six have been acquired by preservation groups.

As the 1960s progressed further designs of main-line diesel locomotives started to arrive from the manufacturers. One of the shortest-lived classes, which began working in Scotland in the autumn of 1962, was the new Clayton Type 1 (Class 17), its centre-cab layout giving it a unique appearance. This was a versatile design, having two Paxman engines, one or both of which could be used, depending upon load. More than 80 examples were allocated to Eastfield and Haymarket, and these were to be seen working singly or in pairs, handling all types of goods trains around the lowlands and central belt of Scotland. With no steam-heating equipment they were seldom used on passenger trains, and even then only during the summer months. Unfortunately it soon became apparent that their engines were developing major technical problems, and although 117 locomotives were built all were rapidly phased out of service, the last

Saturday 20 July 1963
In pristine condition, having been completed the previous month, Brush/Sulzer Type 4 No D1527 stands at the western end of Haymarket depot. Later renumbered 47 423, this locomotive would remain in service until July 1992. *Author*

being withdrawn in 1971. One example survived to pass into industrial use and finally into preservation.

One of the most successful of the later designs started to appear from the manufacturer in the summer of 1962. This was the Brush/Sulzer Type 4 (Class 47), of which more than 500 would be constructed and delivered over a five-year period. The type was first seen in Scotland in 1963, but none was allocated until 1965, when Haymarket received a batch. Soon regarded as efficient and versatile workhorses, they handled all types of traffic, from express passenger to fast fitted goods trains, and were to be seen as far north as Aberdeen, working postal, parcels, goods and passenger trains on both the ex-Caledonian and North British routes into the city. Further south they were used on passenger and goods traffic on the West Coast main line, the East Coast main line, the old 'Sou'West' Nith Valley line into Glasgow and the Waverley route into Edinburgh.

Another design which would eventually become closely associated with Scotland was the English Electric Type 3 (Class 37), introduced in 1960. However, it was not until

1966 that some examples were allocated to Scottish depots, Haymarket (Edinburgh) and Polmadie (Glasgow) being the main recipients. Although not initially seen in large numbers in Scotland, this highly successful class would from the early 1980s become the mainstay of motive power in the north and west of Scotland, replacing Classes 26 and 27.

The final locomotive type to be seen working regularly into Scotland in the 1960s was the later English Electric Type 4 (Class 50), of which only 50 examples were constructed, being delivered in 1967/8. All were allocated to Crewe depot and were used almost exclusively on the Anglo-Scottish passenger and goods traffic north of Crewe until the early 1970s, when they were displaced by the extension of West Coast electrification to Glasgow. All were subsequently transferred to the Western Region, where, due to reliability problems they were progressively refurbished throughout the 1980s. Final withdrawals of the class took place in the early 1990s, and more than a third of the 50 locomotives built have survived to be purchased by preservation groups.

The Highlands and the Far North

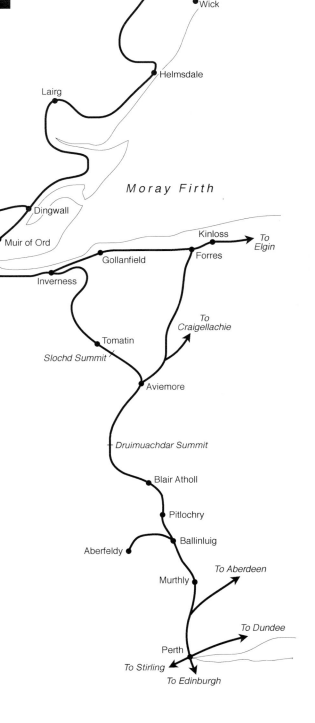

In early 1960 steam still reigned supreme on the ex-Highland Railway line north from Perth to Inverness and thence to the Kyle of Lochalsh and to Wick and Thurso. By the end of 1960 diesel locomotives were starting to displace steam on both passenger and goods traffic on these lines, and by the following summer steam traction would disappear, to be replaced completely by diesel power. In 1959 Metro-Cammell-built DMUs (Class 101) had started to arrive at Perth to operate the Perth–Blair Atholl local passenger services, while in 1960 the first main-line diesels to be allocated to Inverness depot were a couple of English Electric Type 1 (Class 20) and 19 BR/Sulzer Type 2 (Class 24) locomotives. These were followed later in 1960 by 27 BRCW/Sulzer Type 2 (Class 26) locomotives, which soon started handling passenger traffic on the Inverness–Perth route, the Aberfeldy branch and the Inverness–Kyle of Lochalsh line. For a year or so steam and diesel locomotives could be seen working side by side on these routes, often with a diesel piloting a steam locomotive — indeed, for a short period steam and diesel locomotives shared the impressive ex-Highland Railway roundhouse at Inverness — but by the summer of 1961 steam had gone, and the shed itself was closed in June 1962 and later demolished. For the rest of the 1960s and into the early 1970s all the traffic on these ex-Highland lines was handled by BR and BRCW Type 2 diesels.

October 1960
Passing through the beautiful countryside north of Perth, a Metro-Cammell two-car DMU is seen near Murthly on a Blair Atholl–Perth working. *Ian Allan Library*

Wednesday 22 July 1959
At Blair Atholl station, a Metro-Cammell two-car DMU has arrived from Perth. There appears to be a disproportionate number of crew for this service — driver-training? *R. Furness*

Wednesday 14 April 1965

At Ballinluig, BRCW/Sulzer Type 2 No D5321, on the right, attaches a through coach from Aberfeldy, to the 8.40am Struan–Perth train. On the left, similar locomotive No D5336, which brought the train from Struan, transfers to the Aberfeldy branch-line train. Note the tablet-exchange mechanism at the platform end. The branch to Aberfeldy was opened by the Highland Railway in July 1865 and closed just two months short of its 100th anniversary, in May 1965. No D5321 would be withdrawn in October 1991 (as No 26 021) and D5336 two years later (as 26 036). *J. M. French*

Friday 3 April 1964
BR/Sulzer Type 2 No D5114 waits to leave Aberfeldy with the 12.17 mixed train to Ballinluig. This locomotive was not renumbered in the TOPS scheme, being withdrawn following an accident in October 1972. *Ian G. Holt*

Thursday 18 April 1963
BRCW/Sulzer Type 2 No D5336 arrives at Aberfeldy station with the 4.47pm from Ballinluig. *Leslie Sandler*

Monday 22 May 1961
A pair of BR/Sulzer Type 2s, Nos D5126 and D5131, climb to Druimuachdar Summit with the 11.0am Inverness–Perth train. D5126 would be withdrawn in February 1976 as No 24 126, but D5131 was never renumbered in the TOPS scheme, being withdrawn in September 1971 as a result of accident damage sustained earlier in the year. *J. A. Hamilton*

Monday 30 July 1962

BRCW/Sulzer Type 2s Nos D5338 and D5343 at the foot of the climb to Slochd Summit, north of Aviemore, with the 10.0am Glasgow Buchanan Street–Inverness. No D5338 would be withdrawn as No 26 038 in October 1992, whilst D5343, withdrawn as No 26 043 in January 1993 and purchased for preservation, is currently under restoration on the Gloucestershire–Warwickshire Railway. *Anthony A. Vickers*

Thursday 8 September 1960

The 3.45pm Inverness–Glasgow train south of Aviemore with BRCW/Sulzer Type 2 No D5324 in charge. Note the ex-Highland Railway Royal Mail TPO carriage leading; this was built in 1916 and managed to survive until 1961. Withdrawn in October 1992 as No 26 024, the locomotive survives in preservation on the Bo'ness & Kinneil Railway. *J. C. Haydon*

Tuesday 27 August 1963
Approximately two thirds of the line between Inverness and Aberdeen was double-track, the remainder being single-line with a tablet-exchange system in use for express passenger trains. Here a Swindon-built 'Cross-Country' DMU exchanges tablets as it speeds through Kinloss station. The leading coach of this three-car set is No Sc51786. *Author*

Thursday 29 August 1963
Just south of Tomatin station, on the line from Inverness to Aviemore, BRCW/Sulzer Type 2 No D5318 has failed on a goods train heading south for Perth. This locomotive would be withdrawn in January 1982 as No 26 018. *Author*

15

Right:
Monday 26 August 1963
To facilitate express passenger trains' using the single-track lines north of Inverness to Wick, Thurso and Kyle of Lochalsh, a tablet-exchange system was employed. The tablet (or token), contained in a leather pouch, was exchanged before entering a new section. This photograph, taken from a Swindon-built three-car 'Cross-Country' DMU speeding south, shows the exchange taking place at Muir of Ord station. *Author*

Opposite:
Friday 30 April 1971
This excellent photograph shows BR/Sulzer Type 2 No D5123 approaching Muir of Ord with a pickup goods from Wick to Inverness. Note the pair of headlights fitted to this locomotive, which would be withdrawn in July 1976 as No 24 123.
J. H. Cooper-Smith

Monday 9 July 1962

A passenger train from Aberdeen to Inverness crosses the A96 road at the level crossing near Gollanfield on the single-track section of this line. In charge are a pair of BRCW/Sulzer Type 2s, No D5340 leading D5344. The latter would be withdrawn as No 26 044 in January 1984, but D5340, having remained in service (latterly as No 26 040) until December 1992 before sale to a private owner, is currently under restoration. *Author*

**Wednesday
4 September 1968**
BR/Sulzer Type 2 No D5130
arrives at Dingwall station
with the 10.30 train from
Inverness to Wick and Thurso.
Again, note the pair of
headlights fitted to this
locomotive. It was
withdrawn in December
1976 as No 24 130.
D. A. Bosomworth

**Saturday
7 September 1963**
BR/Sulzer Type 2 No D5119
enters Helmsdale station
heading north with a Class 8
goods train. Renumbered
24 119, the locomotive
would be withdrawn in
July 1976. *M. S. Welch*

Friday 3 September 1965
A busy scene at Thurso station as the 11.10 train to Georgemas Junction waits to leave behind BR/Sulzer Type 2 No D5126. This locomotive would be withdrawn from service in February 1976 as No 24 126. *Ian Smith*

Wednesday 7 September 1960
The 3.35pm Wick–Inverness leaves Helmsdale station behind ex-LMS Class 5MT 4-6-0 No 44785, piloted by BR/Sulzer Type 2 No D5118. No 44785 would be withdrawn from service in June 1964, but D5118 would survive (latterly as No 24 118) until December 1976. *E. W. H. Greig*

Wednesday 28 August 1963
The landscape between Dingwall and Kyle of Lochalsh is both rugged and picturesque.
Here BR/Sulzer Type 2 No D5125 negotiates the curves prior to arriving at Garve station.
This locomotive was withdrawn in March 1976 as No 24 125. *Author*

Wednesday 11 July 1962
Near the end of the rugged 63-mile line from Dingwall to Kyle of Lochalsh is the small fishing village of Plockton. The station was a gem, and at the time of this photograph its wooden buildings had just been repainted, all the internal panelling being re-varnished. Here BRCW/Sulzer Type 2 No D5318 prepares to depart on the final stage of its journey. *Author*

Wednesday 26 May 1965
The driver of BRCW/Sulzer Type 2 No D5326 prepares to exchange the single-line token as he enters Garve station with the 10.30 Kyle of Lochalsh–Inverness. Renumbered 26 026, the locomotive would remain in service until January 1992. *Noel A. Machell*

Thursday 13 July 1967

The second man on BRCW/Sulzer Type 2 No D5326 picks up the token from the signalman as the 11.10 to Inverness leaves Kyle of Lochalsh. In the background BR/Sulzer Type 2 No D5050 waits with a goods train. D5326 would survive (as No 26 026) until January 1992, but D5050 (as 24 050) was to succumb as early as October 1975. *Ian Allan Library*

Wednesday 6 September 1961

With the hills of the Isle of Skye towering in the background, BR/Sulzer Type 2 No D5122 shunts a goods train at Kyle of Lochalsh while sister locomotive No D5121 waits to leave with the 10.45am to Inverness. No D5122 was never renumbered in the TOPS scheme, being withdrawn following an accident in October 1968; D5121 would survive until December 1976, by which time it had been renumbered 24 121. *Brian Stephenson*

Thursday 13 July 1967
The hills on Skye loom over
BRCW/Sulzer Type 2
No D5320 as it runs round
its train at Kyle of Lochalsh.
This locomotive was
withdrawn in October 1991
as No 26 028. *C. Lofthus*

Top right:
Tuesday 5 May 1964
Journey's end. BRCW/Sulzer Type 2 No D5322 stands at
Kyle of Lochalsh, having arrived during a heavy rainstorm
with the 10.30 from Inverness. This locomotive would be
withdrawn in February 1981 as No 26 022. *Ian Allan Library*

Lower right:
Friday 8 September 1961
BRCW/Sulzer Type 2 No D5343 shunts on the quay at
Kyle of Lochalsh. Note the cattle wagons in the background,
still very much a part of the railway scene at this time.
Brian Stephenson

Aberdeen and the North East

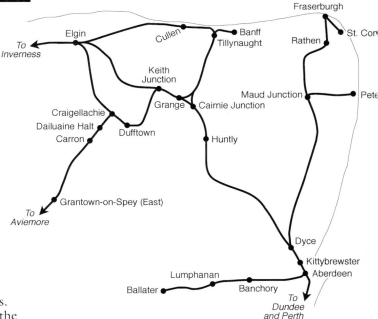

In the early 1960s Aberdeen and the North East of Scotland still held many attractions for a railway enthusiast. The 'Royal Deeside' branch to Ballater, the Buchan branches to Peterhead and Fraserburgh were still open, as were the web of lines serving the towns and villages of Morayshire and Banffshire; this included the beautifully situated line that wound its way along the Banff and Moray coastline serving the fishing villages of Portsoy, Cullen, Portknockie, Findochty and Portessie. It also included the ex-GNSR line from Keith Junction to Elgin via Craigellachie, where there was a junction with the Speyside line to Aviemore. Railbuses were introduced in 1959 on the Elgin–Aviemore Speyside service in an attempt to reduce costs, but this exercise proved only a limited success. Unfortunately, virtually all these lines were closed, the coast line being closed to passenger traffic in July 1964, and that from Keith to Elgin via Craigellachie succumbing in May 1968, but the 10 or so miles between Keith Town and Dufftown survived and has recently been reopened by the Keith & Dufftown Railway, using Derby-built two-car DMUs (Class 108). Passenger services between Elgin and Aviemore via Craigellachie were withdrawn in October 1965. Those from Aberdeen to Peterhead and Fraserburgh ceased respectively in May and October 1965, but goods services survived on the latter branch until the late 1970s.

With the run-down of steam power to the north of Aberdeen during 1960/1, large numbers of NBL/MAN Type 2 (Class 21) diesels were allocated to Kittybrewster depot and could be seen handling most of the passenger traffic to the Buchan branches of Peterhead and Fraserburgh. These locomotives were also used for both passenger and goods traffic on the coast line to Elgin and Forres via Tillynaught. By 1960 four English Electric Type 1 (Class 20) locomotives were allocated to Kittybrewster and were to be seen on fish trains from the Buchan branches. Meanwhile BRCW/Sulzer Type 2s (Class 26) were put to work handling (primarily) passenger trains to Inverness and to the south on Dundee and Edinburgh services. English Electric Type 4s (Class 40) reached Aberdeen with postal, parcels or passenger trains from England via Perth, returning with

similar traffic, and could also be seen working passenger trains such as the 'Aberdonian' to London via Edinburgh.

During 1961 Kittybrewster depot closed to steam locomotives and became the servicing point for diesels working north from the city. Based here were NBL/MAN and BRCW/Sulzer Type 2s and English Electric Type 1 (Class 20) locomotives, along with a handful each of Andrew Barclay-built 0-4-0 diesel-mechanical (Class 06) and BR-built 0-6-0 diesel-electric (Class 08) shunters.

Early morning around Aberdeen harbour would witness a scene of hectic activity, with fishing boats disgorging their catches for the market, but by mid-morning calm would descend and one of the Barclay 0-4-0 shunters could be seen shunting wagons of coal for the gas works or wagonloads of paper pulp for the local paper mills which would be routed through the Waterloo goods yard.

Diesel multiple-units started to arrive in the Aberdeen area in the summer of 1959, when Cravens two-car (Class 105) units were used on the 'Royal Deeside' line to Ballater. These took turns with the unique battery multiple-unit, which saw intermittent use. The branch closed in 1966, but there are currently (2004) plans to reopen a section of the line. Surprisingly the battery multiple-unit survived into preservation, so at some time in the future it may be seen again on this line.

Monday 3 August 1964

This excellent shot shows the approach to Aberdeen Joint station from the north, with the gantry of signals protecting the platforms, as NBL Type 2 No D6150 enters the station at the head of a passenger train from the north. To the right waits the station pilot, EE 0-6-0 diesel-electric shunter No D3932. The Type 2 was withdrawn in December 1967, but the shunter would survive (latterly as 08 764) until May 1988, thereafter being sold for industrial use. *A. H. Wells*

Saturday 16 June 1962
Arriving at Kittybrewster goods yard with a goods train from Keith, NBL/MAN Type 2 No D6143 pilots English Electric Type 1 No D8031. The former would be withdrawn in December 1967, but No D8031 would survive (as 20 031) until October 1989, subsequently passing into preservation on the Keighley & Worth Valley Railway. *S. Creer*

Monday 2 August 1965
BR/Sulzer Type 2 No D5114, fitted with small snowploughs, and BRCW/ Sulzer Type 2 No D5314 are seen stabled at Kittybrewster depot. No D5114 was withdrawn after an accident in October 1972; D5314 (latterly numbered 26 014) would remain in service until October 1992 before passing into preservation on the Caledonian Railway at Brechin. *I. Keast*

Saturday 31 August 1963
English Electric Type 1
No D8031 waits to come on
shed at Kittybrewster depot.
Visible in the background,
working in Kittybrewster
goods yard, is Andrew
Barclay 0-4-0 diesel-
mechanical shunter
No D2416; this locomotive
would be withdrawn in
November 1972. *Author*

Saturday 17 October 1964
Preceded by the pointsman,
Andrew Barclay-built 0-4-0
diesel-mechanical shunter
No D2418 negotiates the
cobbled quayside of
Aberdeen harbour.
The locomotive would be
withdrawn from service in
December 1968. *Author*

Saturday 5 September 1970
BRCW/Sulzer Type 2 No D5309 trundles through Maud Junction station with a Fraserburgh–Aberdeen fish train. The branch from Maud to Peterhead was officially closed to goods traffic two days later, on 7 September, but goods traffic on the branch to Fraserburgh survived until October 1979, thereby outlasting No D5309, which, as No 26 009, was withdrawn from service in January 1977. *Derek Cross*

Wednesday 13 July 1960
English Electric Type 1 No D8031 approaches Rathen with a Class C fast fish train from Fraserburgh to Aberdeen. This locomotive was one of an initial batch of 15 built by Robert Stephenson & Hawthorn, seven of which were allocated to Scotland. *John. A. N. Emslie*

Tuesday 28 June 1966

English Electric Type 1 No D8032 stands at Carron, having arrived with an Aviemore–Craigellachie pickup goods.
Passenger trains had been withdrawn in October 1965, but goods traffic continued for a few more years.
Latterly numbered 20 032, this locomotive was sold to DRS in 1997. *John M. Boyes*

Tuesday 20 June 1967

BR/Sulzer Type 2 No D5132 leaves Craigellachie Junction with the 14.00 Craigellachie–Aviemore pickup goods.
Note the whisky barrels in the wagons — full or empty? Renumbered 24 132, the locomotive was withdrawn from service
in February 1976. *John M. Boyes*

The signalman at Tillynaught
prepares to exchange tokens
with a crew member of
NBL/MAN Type 2 No D6152,
seen at the head of the
2.10pm from Aberdeen to
Elgin and Forres.
Leslie Sandler

Top left:

Friday 15 July 1960
In almost ex-works condition, NBL/MAN Type 2 No D6152
stands outside Fraserburgh shed; inside is classmate
No D6139. These locomotives would be withdrawn
in August 1968 and December 1967 respectively.
John A. N. Emslie

Lower left:

Friday 19 April 1963
A Cravens two-car DMU waits to leave St Combs as the
8.55pm train to Fraserburgh. The branch would close
to all traffic in May 1965. *Leslie Sandler*

Wednesday 22 July 1959
One of five railbuses built by Park Royal and introduced in 1958, No SC79970 prepares to leave Craigellachie as the 7.52am Aviemore–Elgin service. The railbus would finally be withdrawn in March 1967. *R. Furness*

Tuesday 22 August 1961
Another Park Royal-built railbus, No SC79971, arrives at Grantown-on-Spey East with the 2.45pm Elgin–Aviemore service. This example would be withdrawn in February 1968. *J. C. Haydon*

Saturday 11 August 1962
The beautifully situated line between Portsoy and Elgin wound its way along the coastline serving
the fishing villages of Cullen, Portknockie, Findochty and Portessie. This bright summer's day
sees NBL/MAN Type 2 No D6145 leaving Cullen in the background as it heads the 2.10pm from
Aberdeen to Elgin and Forres. This line would close to all traffic in May 1968, but by then the
locomotive had already been withdrawn from service, succumbing in December 1967.
Anthony A. Vickers

Wednesday 21 June 1967
BRCW/Sulzer Type 2
No D5322 between Dailuaine
Halt and Carron station with
the 14.00 pickup goods from
Craigellachie to Aviemore.
The locomotive would be
withdrawn in February 1981
as No 26 022. *John M. Boyes*

Top right:
Monday 10 August 1964
A Cravens two-car DMU leaves Lumphanan station with a
service to Ballater. During the early 1960s services on the
Ballater branch were shared between conventional DMUs
and the unique battery-electric multiple-unit (built in 1958),
which saw only intermittent use; there was also the occasional
steam working. The branch closed to passenger traffic in
February 1966. *A. H. Wells*

Lower right:
Friday 31 July 1964
A Metro-Cammell two-car DMU leaves Banchory station
as the 18.45 service from Ballater to Aberdeen. *A. H. Wells*

Fife, Dundee, Perth and Stirling

Map stations and labels: To Aberdeen, Stonehaven, Carmont, Drumlithie, Bridge of Dun, Montrose, Forfar, To Aviemore, Dundee, Tayport, Wormit, Perth, Crieff, Comrie, Leuchars Junction, St Andrews, Gleneagles, Ladybank, To Oban, Kinross Junction, Thornton Junction, Crail, Rumbling Bridge, Kilconquhar, Pittenweem, Dunblane, Bridge of Allan, Alloa, Cowdenbeath, Kirkcaldy, Stirling, Dunfermline, To Larbert, 1, 2, 3, To Glasgow, To Edinburgh

Key:
1. Inverkeithing
2. North Queensferry
3. Dalmeny

During 1958 the Scottish Region started to receive Metro-Cammell two-car (Class 101) DMUs, some of which were based at Dundee. These soon started operating services between Dundee and Edinburgh via Thornton Junction and Kirkcaldy, as well as between Dundee and Glasgow via Perth; before long they were also displacing some steam workings on the local services to Tayport, Leuchars Junction and St Andrews and being used on services from St Andrews to both Glasgow and Edinburgh via the East Neuk line. Additionally, they could be seen working services from Stirling to Edinburgh via Alloa and Dunfermline. In 1959, in an attempt to reduce costs, British Railways was experimenting with four-wheeled railbuses, and one of these was used on the Devon Valley line between Stirling and Kinross Junction, through services on this route to Perth being operated by Metro-Cammell DMUs. By 1960/1 Edinburgh–Perth/Inverness trains were being hauled by BR/Sulzer Type 2 (Class 24) or BRCW/Sulzer Type 2 (Class 26) diesels working in pairs; Edinburgh–Aberdeen passenger workings were handled by BRCW/Sulzer Type 2s, while through workings from London or the South to Aberdeen would be hauled by an English Electric Type 4 (Class 40).

Goods traffic in Fife was dominated by the coal trade and the movement of large quantities of coal to the cities, towns, ports and power stations around the Firth of Forth. In the early 1960s this was hauled almost entirely by steam power, but the fast through goods services, such as fish trains, between Aberdeen and the south via Edinburgh were very often hauled by

Friday 30 September 1966
English Electric Type 4 No D361 approaches Inverkeithing with the 13.56 Dundee–Edinburgh service.
This locomotive would be withdrawn from service as No 40 161 in December 1980. *C. T. Gifford*

English Electric Type 4 (Class 40) or Brush/Sulzer Type 4 (Class 47) diesel locomotives.

Stirling station is still probably one of the most attractive in Scotland, with its crow-stepped gables and a fine concourse with ornate ironwork supporting a large glazed roof. It has a wide sweeping staircase linking the main station buildings to the remaining platforms by means of a footbridge. During 1960/1 passenger traffic serving the station amounted to more than 80 trains every weekday, while goods, parcels and postal traffic provided the visiting enthusiast with a continually busy and changing scene. During this period much of the traffic was still steam-hauled, but diesel locomotives were becoming more prominent through their use on a large number of passenger trains; those between Glasgow and Oban were hauled by either NBL/MAN (Class 21) or BRCW/Sulzer Type 2s, while those between Glasgow, Perth, Dundee and Aberdeen were also being handled by a variety of Type 2s — BR/Sulzer, NBL/MAN or BRCW/Sulzer — usually working in pairs. Stirling was also the terminus for local stopping trains on the routes to Edinburgh Waverley via Dunfermline and to Perth

via Alloa and the Devon Valley line, both worked by Metro-Cammell two-car DMUs. Through traffic from the South coming off the West Coast main line and heading for Perth and Aberdeen would normally be handled by an English Electric Type 4, although as the decade progressed a greater number of Brush/Sulzer Type 4s would be seen hauling such trains.

By the end of 1961 steam locomotives were no longer used north of Perth on the ex-Highland line to Inverness, and all the services were now operated by BR/Sulzer or BRCW/Sulzer Type 2s, mostly working in pairs. However, on the ex-Caledonian line north of Perth, to Forfar and Aberdeen, steam locomotives were still sharing operations alongside their diesel counterparts on both passenger and goods traffic. Like Stirling, Perth was a very busy station, with over 60 passenger services using the station every weekday. In addition to BR/Sulzer and BRCW/Sulzer Type 2s, NBL/MAN Type 2s and English Electric Type 4s were also to be seen working passenger trains through Perth, while by the mid-1960s Brush/Sulzer Type 4s were appearing in greater numbers.

Above:

Wednesday 5 July 1967

An Aberdeen–Edinburgh express passenger train bursts from the tunnel as it passes North Queensferry station behind Brush/Sulzer Type 4 No D1974 (later 47 273 and then 47 627 *City of Oxford*). This locomotive would last see service in March 2000. *C. F. Burton*

Right:

Thursday 14 July 1960

Seven years earlier, motive power on this service was very different. An Aberdeen–Edinburgh express passes North Queensferry station behind BR/Sulzer Type 2 No D5116. This locomotive would be withdrawn from service in September 1976 as No 24 116. *C. P. Boocock*

Left:

Saturday 29 May 1965

Pausing at North Queensferry station, the 10.33 stopping service from Edinburgh Waverley to Stirling via Dunfermline has just crossed the beautifully balanced structure of the Forth Bridge. The train consists of a pair of two-car Gloucester RCW DMUs (Class 100). *C. W. R. Bowman*

Above:

Thursday 20 February 1964
Having negotiated the steeply graded branch from Kirkcaldy goods yard, Hunslet-built 0-6-0 diesel-mechanical (Class 05) shunter No D2580 stands at the harbour with a very short goods train. This locomotive would be withdrawn in June 1968. *Author*

Left:

Thursday 26 May 1960
Seen pausing for a signal check near Cowdenbeath is a three-car Metro-Cammell DMU providing the 10.50am service from Perth to Edinburgh Waverley.
C. J. Allen

Right:

Saturday 15 September 1962
English Electric Type 4 No D358 powers through the station at Thornton Junction with an express from Aberdeen to Edinburgh. This locomotive would be withdrawn from service in December 1983 as No 40 158. *Author*

Saturday 20 July 1963
Formed of two three-car
Metro-Cammell DMUs,
a Glasgow Queen Street–
Dundee Tay Bridge service
pauses at Kilconquhar
station on the East Neuk line.
All traffic on this line ceased
in October 1969.
John A. N. Emslie

Sunday 21 July 1963
Seen nearing Pittenweem is
the 9.55am Glasgow Queen
Street–Anstruther service,
also provided by two three-
car Metro-Cammell DMUs.
Moray MacWhirter

Monday 22 April 1963
A three-car Metro-Cammell DMU waits to leave Leuchars Junction as the 7.35am service to St Andrews, whilst, on the right, another, similar unit has just arrived from Dundee Tay Bridge with a service for Glasgow Queen Street. *Leslie Sandler*

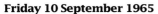

Friday 10 September 1965
A two-car Metro-Cammell DMU constituting the 15.15 service from Dundee Tay Bridge to Tayport pauses at Wormit station.
The remainder of the line, which ran from Tayport to Leuchars Junction, had closed to passengers in January 1956. Wormit station would itself close in May 1969. *C. C. Thorburn*

Saturday 7 March 1964
On the northern approach to the Tay Bridge a Derby three-car DMU (Class 107) on a Dundee–Tayport service
is passed by a northbound goods train headed by ex-LNER Class B1 4-6-0 No 61172.
The 'B1' was withdrawn from service in December 1965. *A. H. Wells*

March 1961
An Edinburgh–Aberdeen passenger train passes Camperdown Junction behind BRCW/Sulzer Type 2s Nos D5302 and D5317. It would appear that the steam-heating connection between the two locomotives has failed. No D5317 would be withdrawn as No 26 017 in August 1977; No D5302 would remain in service (as No 26 002) until October 1992, thereafter passing into private ownership, and is currently under restoration on the Strathspey Railway. *T. Mahoney*

April 1961
Nearing the end of their journey, NBL/MAN Type 2s Nos D6127 and D6135 approach Dundee
with a passenger train from Glasgow. Both locomotives would be withdrawn from service
in December 1967. *T. Mahoney*

Tuesday 8 June 1965
English Electric Type 4
No D363 passes Dundee
MPD with a Class 3 goods
train for Edinburgh.
In the background ex-LNER
Class B1 4-6-0 No 61293
simmers outside the shed.
The 'B1' would be withdrawn
from service in August 1966,
whereas the Type 4 No D363
would survive (latterly as
40 163) until June 1982.
L. A. Nixon

Left:
**Thursday
2 September 1965**
An Aberdeen–Edinburgh passenger train approaches Drumlithie, near Stonehaven, hauled by English Electric Type 4 No D260. Withdrawn from normal service in January 1985 as No 40 060, this locomotive would pass into departmental stock as No 97 405, being finally withdrawn in March 1987. *P. Hocquard*

Right:
**Thursday
2 September 1965**
A southbound fast fitted Class 3 goods from Aberdeen seen near Carmont, hauled by English Electric Type 4 No D365. This locomotive would be withdrawn from service in July 1981 as No 40 165. *P. Hocquard*

Left:
Friday 8 July 1966
The 17.15 Aberdeen–Glasgow relief passes Bridge of Dun behind BR/Sulzer Type 2 No D5126. Passenger traffic here ceased in September 1967; the four-mile branch to Brechin (left foreground) was finally closed to goods traffic in May 1981 and is nowadays operated by the Caledonian Railway from its base in Brechin. Latterly numbered 24 126, No D5126 would be withdrawn from service in February 1976. *John M. Boyes*

Left:
**Thursday
2 September 1965**
Brush/Sulzer Type 4
No D1847 (later renumbered
47 197) passes Carmont,
just south of Stonehaven,
with the up afternoon postal
from Aberdeen to Glasgow.
At the time of writing this
locomotive remains active
with Freightliner.
P. Hocquard

Top right:
**Saturday
8 September 1962**
Headed by English Electric
Type 4 No D366, an
Inverness–Edinburgh
passenger train passes
Hilton Junction, near Perth.
Renumbered 40 166, the
locomotive would be
withdrawn in February 1982.
Derek Cross

Lower right:
**Thursday
12 September 1963**
The 4.0pm from Dundee
West to Glasgow Buchanan
Street draws into the
platform at Perth General
behind BR/Sulzer Type 2
No D5124. This locomotive
would be withdrawn in
December 1976 as No 24 124.
T. Mahoney

Monday 30 May 1966
Brush/Sulzer Type 4 No D1540 emerges from the north end of Moncrieff Tunnel, approaching Perth
with the 07.50 London King's Cross–Perth Anglo-Scottish car-carrier. Renumbered 47 013,
this locomotive would be withdrawn from service in February 1987. *C. W. R. Bowman*

Wednesday 21 June 1961
The 'Bon Accord' from Glasgow Buchanan Street to Aberdeen approaches Perth behind a pair of NBL/MAN Type 2s (Class 21), Nos D6107 and D6126. The former would be re-engined and redesignated as a Class 29, surviving in this form until October 1971, but No D6126 would be withdrawn in April 1968. *Stuart Chambers*

Wednesday 23 June 1965
Standing in Perth station at the head of a Perth–Edinburgh service are a pair of Sulzer-engined Type 2s — BRCW No D5320 and BR-built No D5124. Note the detail of the tablet-exchange mechanism fitted to the cabside of the latter. No D5320 would survive (latterly as 26 028) until October 1991, but No D5124 would be withdrawn (as No 24 124) in December 1976. *D. L. Percival*

Friday 3 June 1966
This open vista looking south shows the approach to Perth station with the (then) new signalbox. Re-engined NBL Type 2 No D6114 is nearing the station at the head of the 09.15 Glasgow Buchanan Street–Dundee passenger train. This locomotive would be withdrawn in October 1971. *C. W. R. Bowman*

Top left:
Monday 18 June 1962
English Electric Type 4 No D262 leaves Perth at the head of the up car-carrier/sleeper to London King's Cross. The locomotive, here is in almost 'as built' condition, with gangway connection, disc indicators and no yellow warning panel, would be withdrawn from service in November 1981 as No 40 062. *P. J. Lynch*

Lower left:
Monday 20 July 1964
The 10.30 Inverness–Glasgow Buchanan Street leaves Perth behind BRCW/Sulzer Type 2 No D5332. Renumbered 26 032, this locomotive was to survive until October 1993. *S. Rickard*

Saturday 27 June 1964
BR/Sulzer 'Peak' Type 4 No D132 nears Gleneagles station with the 12.00 Dundee West–Glasgow Buchanan Street passenger train. This locomotive would be withdrawn from service (as No 45 075) in January 1985. *W. G. Sumner*

Friday 13 July 1962
At the time of this photograph passengers on the branch from Crieff to Comrie were served by a four-wheeled railbus, No SC79967 being seen arriving at Crieff station. Introduced in 1958, this was one of five built by D. Wickham & Co. The line was the remaining stump of the very picturesque Perth–Balquhidder line skirting Loch Earn, the majority of which had closed to passenger traffic in 1951. The Crieff–Comrie section would close to all traffic in January 1965. *Author*

Tuesday 11 August 1964
A northbound goods train hauled by BRCW/Sulzer Type 2 No D5327, seen near Dunblane. Latterly numbered 26 027, this locomotive would remain in service until July 1991. *Derek Cross*

Sunday 4 July 1965
BRCW/Sulzer Type 2 No D5348 approaches Dunblane from the Perth line with a train containing postal carriages. In the background, swinging away to the left, is the line to Callander and Oban. The section between Dunblane and Crianlarich (Lower) closed suddenly in September 1965 after a severe landslide affected the line near Glenoglehead. Renumbered 27 002, No D5348 would survive until January 1986. *Ian G. Holt*

Wednesday 29 July 1964
A Glasgow–Inverness passenger train approaches Bridge of Allan, hauled by a pair of BRCW/Sulzer Type 2s, Nos D5320 and D5328. The latter was withdrawn in July 1972 after an accident but D5320 would survive until October 1991 as No 26 028 — curiously the identity D5328 would likely have adopted but for its misfortune. *Derek Cross*

Saturday 1 August 1964
BRCW/Sulzer Type 2 No D5328 again, here climbing to Kippenross Tunnel, near Bridge of Allan, with an Edinburgh–Oban passenger train. *A. J. Wheeler*

Saturday 8 August 1959
One of only 20 examples of a unique Pilot Scheme Co-Bo design, Metropolitan-Vickers Type 2 (later Class 28) No D5713 powers out of Stirling, heading south with a passenger train for Glasgow. Note the locomotive shed in the background, with several vintage ex-Caledonian locomotives in the yard. In contrast No D5713 was at this time a stranger to Scotland, being allocated to Derby (17A), but by the early 1960s pairs of Co-Bos could regularly be seen working the 'Condor' overnight goods service from London to Glasgow. However, the design was not deemed a success, and No D5713 would be withdrawn in December 1967.
M. R. Galley

Sunday 4 July 1965
A pair of BRCW/Sulzer Type 2s, No D5364 leading No D5356, coast into Stirling with the 13.30 Aberdeen – Glasgow. Both locomotives would remain in service until 1986, No D5356 (latterly numbered 27 010) being withdrawn in April and No D5364 (27 018) following in May. *Ian G. Holt*

Monday 30 March 1964
With the splendid Wallace Monument in the background, a two-car Metro-Cammell DMU leaves the Alloa line on the approach to Stirling. The leading vehicle is No SC56382. *Paul Riley*

Saturday 30 May 1964
Before closure, the service from Stirling to Perth via the Devon Valley line was reduced to one through train each way per day. The line between Alloa and Kinross Junction had been opened in sections between 1863 and 1871 and traversed the beautiful rolling countryside of Clackmannanshire and Kinross-shire, serving villages with names such as Dollar, Crook of Devon and Rumbling Bridge. Here a two-car Metro-Cammell DMU pauses at Rumbling Bridge station. The line would close to passenger traffic the following month. *J. Spencer Gilks*

Wednesday 4 March 1964
A two-car Metro-Cammell DMU forming the 13.40 Dollar–Stirling service leaves the Devon Valley line
at Alloa East Junction. Bringing up the rear is car No SC51450. *S. Rickard*

Wednesday 4 March 1964
NBL 0-4-0 diesel-hydraulic shunter No D2710 leaves the Devon Valley line at Alloa East Junction with a local goods train.
This locomotive had been numbered 11710 prior to 1957 and would be withdrawn in March 1967. *S. Rickard*

Edinburgh Waverley

The North British Railway completed construction of Waverley station in its present form in 1897, while the imposing North British Hotel was opened in 1902. The station was essentially a huge island area with 19 platforms and two additional suburban platforms, East Coast expresses using the through platforms (1/19 and 10/11) and all other passenger traffic the 15 bay platforms.

By 1960 the western end of the station was seeing the arrival and departure of trains to Glasgow Queen Street, worked by Swindon-built six-car DMUs (later Class 126). These had replaced steam-hauled stock early in 1957 and operated an intensive service, trains departing for Glasgow virtually every half hour throughout the day from 6.30am. Stopping services to Stirling, Perth, Dundee and the Fife coast and on the branch to Corstorphine were provided by Metro-Cammell two-car DMUs (Class 101). Locomotive-hauled passenger trains to Dundee, Aberdeen, Perth and Inverness would be hauled by pairs of Sulzer-engined Type 2s — BR (Class 24) or BRCW (Class 26) — and through trains from the south to Aberdeen by English Electric Type 4s (Class 40).

The eastern end of the station saw the arrival and departure of the named East Coast expresses, a few still steam-hauled but an increasing number worked by English Electric Type 4 diesels. Branch-line trains from this end of the station served Peebles, Galashiels, Musselburgh and North Berwick using Gloucester RCW two-car DMUs (Class 100) introduced during 1958; the service to Musselburgh lasted until September 1964, that to Peebles ceasing earlier, in February 1962. By the summer of 1962 the powerful English Electric 'Deltic' Type 5s (Class 55) were operating a larger number of the named East Coast expresses and the new Brush/Sulzer Type 4s (Class 47) were starting to appear on stopping trains over the same route. The east end of the station also saw the arrival and departure of trains to the South, traversing the Waverley route to Carlisle, and the through train from Leeds and London St Pancras would arrive behind a BR/Sulzer 'Peak' Type 4 (Class 45 or 46). Given the intensive Inner Circle and Outer Circle suburban services using Platforms 20 and 21 and the continual arrival of steam-hauled trains of empty coaching stock from Craigentinny, this end of the station had an air of constant activity.

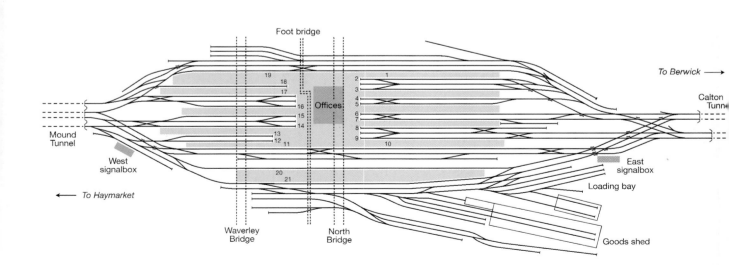

Tuesday 17 May 1966

With a plume of smoke characteristic of a 'Deltic' departure, English Electric Type 5 No D9010, by now named
The King's Own Scottish Borderer, leaves the eastern end of the station at the head of a southbound passenger train.
Latterly numbered 55 010, this locomotive would be withdrawn from service in December 1981. *Author*

Monday 22 July 1963

A splendid view of the west end of Waverley station, featuring BR/Sulzer Type 2 No D5117 and BRCW/Sulzer Type 2 No D5342
leaving with the 4.19pm to Inverness. Note the west-end station pilot shunting in the background. No D5117 would be
withdrawn (as No 24 117) in February 1976, No D5342 surviving (as 26 042) until October 1992. *J. S. Whiteley*

Top right:
Friday 12 June 1964
The 'Queen of Scots' Pullman leaves for Glasgow behind a solitary BRCW/Sulzer Type 2 No D5351. Renumbered 27 005, this locomotive would be withdrawn in July 1987, thereafter passing into preservation on the Bo'ness & Kinneil Railway. *Author*

Left:
Monday 8 February 1965
The BR/Sulzer 'Peak' Type 4s were regular visitors to Edinburgh on the through train from London St Pancras. This would work over the spectacular Waverley route traversing the borders, stopping at such towns as Hawick and Galashiels. Here No D188 has successfully completed its duty as it arrives at Waverley station. This locomotive would be withdrawn as No 46 051 in November 1983. *Author*

Lower right:
Saturday 11 June 1966
Brush/Sulzer Type 4 No D1987 (later renumbered 47 285) waits to leave Waverley's Platform 1 with (according to the headcode) a stopping service for Hawick and Carlisle. Withdrawn in January 1999, this locomotive is currently stored by Fragonset pending a possible return to service. *Author*

Top left:

Thursday 14 July 1960

Another splendid view of the station's western approaches, with a Swindon-built six-car 'Inter-City' DMU departing as the 6.0pm service to Glasgow Queen Street. These units had been introduced on the Edinburgh–Glasgow route early in 1957. Four cars from this class have survived and are in the care of the Scottish Railway Preservation Society (SRPS) at Bo'ness. *C. P. Boocock*

Right:

Friday 9 June 1972

A train of cement tanks bound for Dunbar heads through Princes Street Gardens as it approaches Waverley behind BRCW/Sulzer Type 2 No D5301. Latterly numbered 26 001, this locomotive would remain in service until October 1993 before passing into preservation on the Lakeside & Haverthwaite Railway. *J. H. Cooper-Smith*

Lower left:

Wednesday 22 August 1962

A busy scene at the eastern end of the station, as English Electric Type 4 No D271 departs with the 11.40am Anglo-Scottish car-carrier. Running alongside is a two-car Gloucester DMU operating the 11.35am train from Waverley to Rosewell & Hawthornden; the passenger service to this destination would last for only a few more weeks, ceasing with effect from 10 September. No D271 would survive (latterly as 40 071) until September 1980. *Anthony A. Vickers*

Top left:
Wednesday 29 June 1966
Approaching Waverley station, English Electric Type 4
No D263 passes through Princes Street Gardens with an
Aberdeen–Edinburgh train. This locomotive would be
withdrawn in April 1984 as No 40 063. *Derek Cross*

Lower left:
Saturday 3 July 1965
Having left Waverley station, English Electric Type 4 No D265
passes through Princes Street Gardens as it heads north with
a passenger train for Aberdeen. Note the four-character
headcode panel, which had replaced the earlier discs upon
overhaul. This locomotive would be withdrawn in November
1981 as No 40 065. *David C. Smith*

Saturday 11 July 1964
The down 'Flying Scotsman'
reaches journey's end at
Waverley behind (as yet
un-named) English Electric
Type 5 No D9010. *Author*

Around Edinburgh

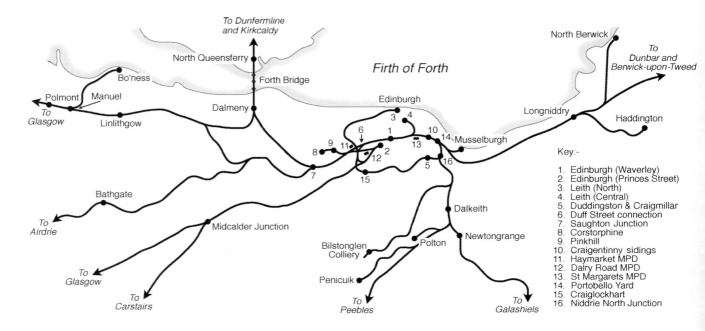

To Dunfermline and Kirkcaldy

North Berwick

To Dunbar and Berwick-upon-Tweed

North Queensferry

Firth of Forth

Bo'ness

Forth Bridge

Polmont | Manuel

Edinburgh

Dalmeny

Longniddry

Haddington

To Glasgow

Linlithgow

Musselburgh

Key:-

1. Edinburgh (Waverley)
2. Edinburgh (Princes Street)
3. Leith (North)
4. Leith (Central)
5. Duddingston & Craigmillar
6. Duff Street connection
7. Saughton Junction
8. Corstorphine
9. Pinkhill
10. Craigentinny sidings
11. Haymarket MPD
12. Dalry Road MPD
13. St Margarets MPD
14. Portobello Yard
15. Craiglockhart
16. Niddrie North Junction

Bathgate

To Airdrie

Midcalder Junction

Dalkeith

Bilstonglen Colliery

Polton

Newtongrange

To Glasgow

Penicuik

To Carstairs

To Peebles

To Galashiels

From the late 1950s enthusiasts visiting Haymarket depot (64B), on Edinburgh's western fringes, could witness the growing number of diesel locomotives being delivered and allocated there. The list of types grew as the 1960s progressed, English Electric Type 4 (Class 40), English Electric Type 5 (Class 55), Brush/Sulzer Type 4 (Class 47), BRCW/Sulzer Type 2 (Class 26), English Electric Type 1 (Class 20) and Clayton Type 1 (Class 17) all working from the depot during the early part of the decade. By the end of 1963 the diesels had taken over completely and steam had been banished from the depot. In the later 1960s several BR/Sulzer Type 2 (Class 24) and English Electric Type 3 (Class 37) locomotives were also allocated.

Following the closure of Haymarket to steam, St Margarets depot (64A) became the main steam depot in Edinburgh, but it too had an allocation of diesel locomotives, albeit only shunters — mainly NBL-built diesel-hydraulic 0-4-0 and BR-built 0-6-0 diesel-electric (Class 08) types. On Sundays, when most of the goods yards around the city

were closed, the up side of the depot would be packed with these shunters, neatly parked around the small turntable.

Dalry Road depot (64C) supplied motive power for the ex-Caledonian Railway line into Princes Street station and remained a stronghold of steam until its closure in October 1965. It had a couple of 0-6-0 diesel-electric shunters allocated for use in goods yards such as Lothian Road, adjacent to Princes Street station, but never anything larger.

The suburban passenger network serving Edinburgh, known locally as 'the Sub', may not have had anywhere near the route mileage of the much larger Glasgow system but nevertheless served well the suburbs to the south and east of the city. Additionally, the branches to Corstorphine, Musselburgh, North Berwick and the border towns of Peebles and Galashiels were all included in the 'suburban' services operated from Waverley station. During 1958 suburban trains on these routes were gradually turned over to DMUs with the introduction of Gloucester RCW two-car sets (Class 100)

and the withdrawal of the steam-hauled stock. All of these passenger services, except those on the North Berwick branch, were withdrawn during the 1960s — the Peebles/Galashiels service in February 1962, the suburban Inner Circle and Outer Circle in September of the same year, the Musselburgh service in September 1964 and the Corstorphine branch from 1 January 1968. One other Edinburgh suburban service 'dieselised' during 1958 was that between Princes Street station and Leith North, withdrawn in April 1962.

Many branch lines around Edinburgh had lost their passenger services during the 1940s and '50s and so never saw DMUs on passenger duties. However, the branches to Balerno, Dalkeith, Gullane, Haddington, Penicuik and Polton all retained goods services well into the late 1960s, and, although most of these were steam-hauled, diesel locomotives such as Clayton Type 1s did reach the likes of Penicuik in the later 1960s.

Wednesday 23 November 1966
The passenger service on the Penicuik branch may have ceased in September 1951, but there was still a twice-daily goods train to Penicuik from Millerhill yard. Several paper mills were still operating in the Esk Valley, the largest of which, at Penicuik, received esparto grass and wood pulp from Granton harbour and Leith Docks in Edinburgh. Here Clayton Type 1 No D8584 has arrived with such a train, and the shunter is preparing for the shunt. The branch was finally closed in March 1967, and the locomotive did not survive much longer, being withdrawn in October 1968.
C. Lofthus

Saturday 27 March 1965
With the remains of a recent snowfall on the ground, BRCW/Sulzer Type 2 No D5315 powers away from Duddingston & Craigmillar station heading west with a goods train. Renumbered 26 015, the locomotive would survive until June 1991. *Author*

Top right:
Wednesday 29 July 1964
Having returned from St Leonard's coal depot in Edinburgh with a solitary brake van, BR/EE 0-6-0 diesel-electric shunter No D3880 stands in the station yard at Duddingston & Craigmillar. Renumbered 08 713, this locomotive would survive until June 1998. *Author*

Lower right:
Saturday 31 March 1962
A Gloucester RCW two-car DMU pauses at Duddingston & Craigmillar station, where it will reverse to the 'Outer Circle' platform before leaving for Musselburgh via Waverley station. *G. M. Staddon / N. E. Stead collection*

Saturday 22 May 1965
Passenger services had been withdrawn from Edinburgh's
Inner Circle and Outer Circle suburban routes in September
1962, but these lines continued as the main arteries for goods
traffic avoiding the city centre. Here English Electric Type 4
No D366 speeds west away from Duddingston & Craigmillar
station at the head of a Class 4 train of cement tank wagons.
The locomotive would be withdrawn in February 1982
as No 40 166. *Author*

Wednesday 8 April 1964
The up 'Queen of Scots'
Pullman passes Saughton
Junction behind BRCW/Sulzer
Type 2 No D5308.
In the background can be
seen the carriage sidings,
which appear to contain
large numbers of Gresley-
and Thompson-designed
coaches. As No 26 008 the
locomotive was to remain in
service until March 1993.
Anthony A. Vickers

Saturday 25 August 1962
With shunting pole in hand,
the Duddingston yard
shunter climbs aboard
BR/English Electric 0-6-0
No D3890 in preparation for
some work. This locomotive
would be withdrawn in
March 1987 as No 08 722.
Author

Monday 31 August 1964
Musselburgh station a few days prior to closure, with a Gloucester two-car DMU preparing to leave with the 18.08 service for Edinburgh Waverley. The leading car is No SC56307. *David C. Smith*

Saturday 28 April 1962
Passengers board the last passenger train to leave Leith North station — the 6.45pm service for Princes Street. Gloucester two-car DMUs had operated the service since May 1958, when they replaced steam-hauled stock. The only surviving remnant from this scene is the station building visible in the background, nowadays used as commercial premises. *W. S. Sellar*

**Saturday
30 December 1967**
At Pinkhill station, on the
Corstorphine branch, a
two-car Metro-Cammell DMU
pauses before proceeding
to Corstorphine. *Author*

**Saturday
30 December 1967**
On the last day of passenger
services on the Corstorphine
branch, a two-car Metro-
Cammell DMU awaits the
'off' with a service for
Edinburgh Waverley. *Author*

Above:

Wednesday 22 August 1962

Inner and Outer Circle suburban-line trains — both formed of Gloucester two-car DMUs — pass at Craigentinny crossover; the leading car of that nearer the camera is No SC56304. Both services, serving stations on the outer edges of Edinburgh, were withdrawn on 10 September 1962. *Anthony A. Vickers*

Left:

Saturday 3 November 1962

An unidentified ex-LNER Class B1 4-6-0 waits to leave Craigentinny carriage sidings with a train of empty coaching stock for Waverley station as English Electric Type 4 No D244 hurries past at the head of a passenger train bound for the same destination. Renumbered 40 044, the latter would remain in service until January 1985. *Author*

Right:

Saturday 20 July 1963

Making what your author believes to have been the first visit to Haymarket depot of a Brush/Sulzer Type 4, No D1527, gleaming in ex-works condition, stands at the western end of the shed. However, not until 1965 did the depot receive an allocation, supplementing its existing English Electric Type 4s. This locomotive would be withdrawn in July 1992 as No 47 423. *Author*

Friday 16 July 1965
Dalry Road depot was very
much a traditional
Caledonian Railway building.
Only in the final year of its
existence did it see any
diesel activity, and even then
only rarely. Clayton Type 1
No D8587, seen in front
of an unidentified classmate,
would be withdrawn in
October 1971. *Author*

Sunday 2 April 1961
BR/English Electric 0-6-0
shunter No D3732 at work
in Portobello goods yard.
In the background can be
seen two interesting old
coaches in use as mess and
tool vans. The locomotive
would be withdrawn in July
1993 as No 08 565. *Author*

Sunday 31 March 1963
Stabled around the small turntable at St Margarets depot, a collection of diesel shunters including unclassified NBL 0-4-0 No D2747, which locomotive would be withdrawn in August 1967. *Author*

Wednesday 5 April 1967
BRCW/Sulzer Type 2 No D5302 negotiates the Duff Street connection with the 10.45 Edinburgh Waverley–Birmingham New Street. Withdrawn in October 1992 as No 26 002, this locomotive is currently to be found on the Strathspey Railway. *Anthony A. Vickers*

Monday 4 July 1966
BR/Sulzer Type 4 No D19 approaches Niddrie North Junction with a train for Carlisle. This locomotive would be withdrawn from service in May 1981 as No 45 025. *Author*

Sunday 30 August 1964
English Electric Type 4
No D229 *Saxonia* approaches
Craiglockhart at the head of
the 10.55 Edinburgh
Waverley–Birmingham
New Street. Renumbered
40 029, this locomotive would
be withdrawn in April 1984.
W. S. Sellar

Friday 1 September 1961
The up 'Queen of Scots'
Pullman passes Polmont
station on its way to
Edinburgh behind
English Electric Type 4
No D262. Standing at the bay
platform is a two-car
Gloucester DMU waiting to
leave for Larbert. No D262
would be withdrawn
in November 1981
as No 40 062. *S. Rickard*

Dunbar

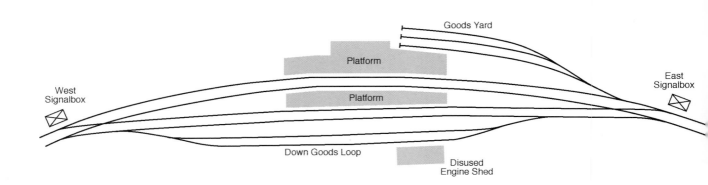

West Signalbox

Goods Yard

Platform

Platform

East Signalbox

Down Goods Loop

Disused Engine Shed

Dunbar, an East Lothian town, fishing harbour and seaside resort, is famous for the Bass Rock Bird Sanctuary (just off the coast), its ancient brewery — 'Dudgeon' (now 'Belhaven') — with its equally famous ales and trademark, and the gently rolling farmland around the town. Dunbar station, on the East Coast main line, is 29 miles from Edinburgh and lies on a long sweeping curve. On the day the author visited — Wednesday 7 July 1965 — the timetable still showed a service of six stopping trains from Edinburgh, including the 'North Briton' to London. All other non-stop express passenger and goods trains by-passed the station platforms by using the main up and down running lines situated behind the down platform.

By 1965 all the main express and stopping passenger trains on the East Coast main line were hauled by diesel traction. The majority of the named expresses were in the hands of English Electric 'Deltic' Type 5s (Class 55), with English Electric Type 4s (Class 40) and Brush/Sulzer Type 4s (Class 47) handling most of the rest. Goods trains were hauled by a variety of locomotives, with steam still seeing an occasional turn. English Electric and Brush/Sulzer Type 4s, along with English Electric Type 1s (Class 20) and Clayton Type 1s (Class 17), working in pairs, were to be seen on a variety of goods workings. The goods yard hosted a little traffic — mostly wagons awaiting entry to the local cement works. Dunbar had a sub-shed allocation from St Margarets in Edinburgh, but by 1965 the shed building on the down side of the line had been demolished and the track lifted.

Top right:
Wednesday 7 July 1965
Brush/Sulzer Type 4 No D1541 pauses at the up platform with a southbound stopping passenger train, its shed-code plate (34G) denoting allocation to Finsbury Park depot. This locomotive would be withdrawn from service in January 1987 as No 47 429. *Author*

Lower right:
Wednesday 7 July 1965
Clayton Type 1s Nos D8577 and D8580 head south with a long Class 8 goods. No D8577 would be withdrawn in March 1969 and No D8580 in October 1971. *Author*

Wednesday 7 July 1965
Brush Type 2 No D5837 hurries past Dunbar station
at the head of a passenger train bound for Edinburgh.
In common with the rest of its class this locomotive
was a stranger to Scotland but would survive in service
(as No 31 304) until September 1998. *Author*

Wednesday 7 July 1965
English Electric 'Deltic'
Type 5 No D9010 passes
with the up 'Flying
Scotsman'. Later named
*The King's Own Scottish
Borderer* and later still
renumbered 55 010, this
locomotive would be
withdrawn from service in
December 1981. *Author*

The Waverley Route

W hen railway enthusiasts talk today about the 'Waverley route', memories of hard working steam locomotives tackling the heavily graded line with its long stretches at 1 in 70 and 1 in 75 come to mind. But from the late 1950s until its closure in 1969 diesel locomotives were to be seen in increasing numbers, sharing duties with their steam counterparts. By 1960 passenger traffic on the line between Carlisle and Edinburgh consisted of five or so trains each way per day, with a couple of through workings from Leeds and London St Pancras. Additionally, there were a handful of local workings from Edinburgh to Hawick and a couple of Carlisle to Hawick locals each day. These were mainly steam-hauled, but the through workings to/from London quickly saw the use of BR/Sulzer 'Peak' Type 4s (Class 45 or 46), and some of the Hawick locals to/from Edinburgh Waverley were being hauled by BRCW/Sulzer Type 2s (Class 26).

Passenger traffic on the Waverley route was only the tip of the iceberg, for increasing numbers of goods trains were using this route into Edinburgh and the central belt of Scotland. This was particularly highlighted when the two modern marshalling yards at Carlisle Kingmoor and Millerhill in Edinburgh were brought into use in 1963. Alongside a wide variety of steam locomotives hauling these goods trains were an increasing number of diesel locomotives. English Electric Type 4s (Class 40) were often seen on through goods trains heading for Carlisle and the South, whilst the newly arrived Clayton Type 1 (Class 17), although deemed unreliable, were regularly seen working in pairs on this route, hauling goods traffic between Kingmoor and Millerhill yards; they could also be seen on pickup goods from Hawick and Galashiels to Edinburgh and on coal trains from the pits around Newtongrange. Another class used increasingly on both passenger and goods trains by the mid-1960s was the Brush/Sulzer Type 4 (Class 47).

By the time of its closure in January 1969 the route had given good service to its local residents, especially those in the towns in its northern half, from Hawick and Galashiels to Edinburgh. The campaign to prevent its closure was both long and vociferous but ultimately failed.

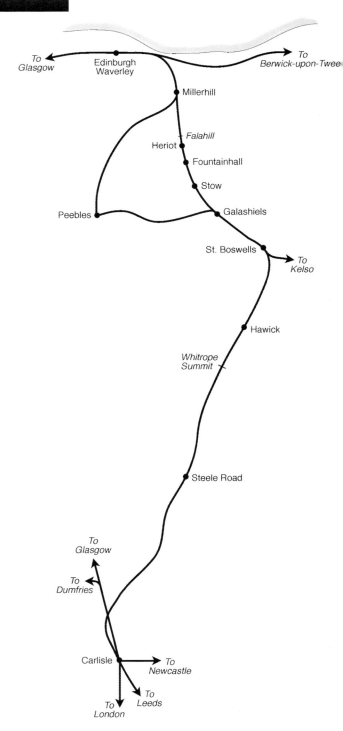

Tuesday 22 November 1966

English Electric Type 4 No D271 waits at the south end of Millerhill yard as Clayton Type 1 No D8560 leaves the Waverley route with a Class 8 goods. No D8560 would be withdrawn in February 1969, No D271 surviving (latterly as 40 071) until September 1980. *C. Lofthus*

Monday 9 September 1968

In overcast conditions an unidentified BR/Sulzer 'Peak' Type 4 speeds through Fountainhall with an express from Edinburgh via Carlisle to the London Midland Region. The locomotive shedcode plate (55A) denotes allocation to Leeds Holbeck depot.
Andrew Muckley

Thursday 3 June 1965

An unidentified English
Electric Type 4 threads its
way through picturesque
countryside near Stow with a
northbound Class 4 goods.
The rebuilt headcode panel
suggests the locomotive
to be one of the original
Haymarket-allocated batch,
Nos D260-6. *Derek Cross*

Top right:

Thursday 5 September 1963

English Electric Type 4 No D214 *Antonia* heading south near
Falahill with a train of lorry chassis from Bathgate to Oxford.
Renumbered 40 014, this locomotive would be withdrawn
from service in November 1981. *Derek Cross*

Lower right:

Saturday 25 June 1966

Another unidentified English Electric Type 4 passes
Fountainhall with a train of military equipment heading from
Aberdeen to Chippenham. This locomotive is one of the later
series (Nos D345-99) built with alpha-numeric headcode
displays. *Derek Cross*

Wednesday 29 June 1966
Clayton Type 1s Nos D8570
and D8578 power out of
Steele Road station with a
northbound Class 4 goods.
No D8570 would be
withdrawn in November
1968, No D8578 in May 1969.
Derek Cross

Top left:
Saturday 13 March 1965
Climbing northbound to Whitrope Summit on a Class 4 goods
train are Clayton Type 1s Nos D8575 (leading) and D8574.
The former would be withdrawn in October 1968, the latter
outlasting it by exactly three years. *Paul Riley*

Lower left:
June 1966
The rare sight of Claytons on passenger work: Nos D8523
and D8520 near Fountainhall in charge of a Blackpool–Dundee
special. Both locomotives would be withdrawn in October
1968. *Derek Cross*

Monday 17 May 1965
A two-car Gloucester enters a very wet Galashiels from the north. The only surviving feature from this photograph is the Abbotsford Arms Hotel in the background, the trackbed and the station site now being occupied by a road by-passing the town centre. *Author*

Top left:
Thursday 27 July 1967
BRCW/Sulzer Type 2 (Class 26) No D5301 arrives at Galashiels station with the 14.45 Edinburgh Waverley – Carlisle. Latterly numbered 26 001, this locomotive would be withdrawn in October 1993 and is now preserved on the Lakeside & Haverthwaite Railway. *C. Lofthus*

Lower left:
Friday 5 August 1960
A Gloucester two-car DMU leaves Peebles station with a service for Edinburgh Waverley. Passenger services on this branch were withdrawn in February 1962. *Author*

Around Glasgow

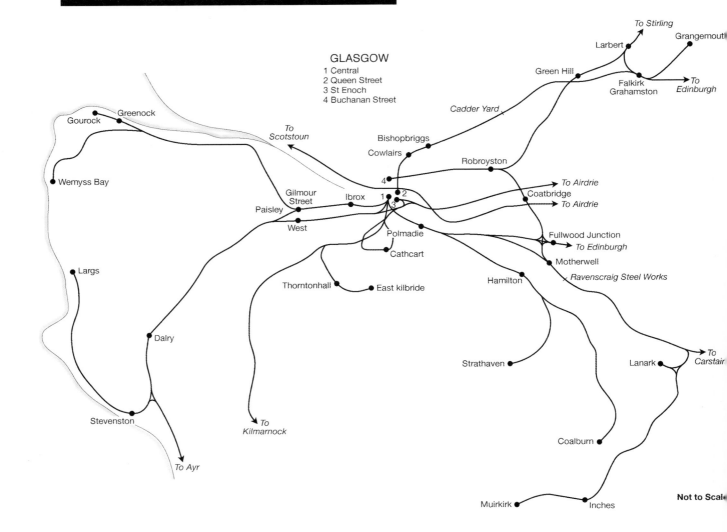

GLASGOW
1 Central
2 Queen Street
3 St Enoch
4 Buchanan Street

Not to Scale

'Dieselisation' of passenger traffic around Glasgow began early in 1957 with the introduction of Swindon-built six-car DMUs (Class 126) on services between Queen Street and Edinburgh Waverley. This successful changeover from steam traction was quickly followed (in 1958) by the introduction of Metro-Cammell two-car DMUs (Class 101) on some services between Buchanan Street and Dundee via both the Perth and Thornton Junction routes. During 1959 Cravens two-car DMUs (Class 105) were introduced on the Cathcart Circle and the second batch of Swindon-built six-car units was delivered for use on services from St Enoch to Ayr, Girvan, Stranraer and Ardrossan and Largs. In 1960 Derby-built three-car DMUs (Class 107) started to arrive in the Glasgow area, primarily for use on the South Side suburban services.

Branch lines in the Glasgow area that survived until the mid-1960s included the very rural lines to Strathaven, Coalburn and Muirkirk, passenger services on these being operated by Cravens, Gloucester (Class 100) or Metro-Cammell two-car DMUs. The Scottish Region Winter Timetable for 1964/5 shows that services

Sunday 4 June 1961
Off-duty Andrew Barclay
0-4-0 diesel-mechanical
shunter No D2433 stands
between a pair of 0-6-0
diesel-electric shunters
at Polmadie depot.
This locomotive would be
withdrawn in June 1972.
Author

on the Strathaven and Coalburn branches were sparse, traffic being generally northbound to Glasgow in the morning and southbound in the afternoon; both branches closed to passenger traffic from October 1965. On the other hand, Muirkirk was quite well served from Lanark, with six or seven trains each way per day to either Douglas West or Muirkirk itself, but, given the area's sparse population, this branch closed to passenger traffic from October 1964.

Another branch near Glasgow operating a very localised service was that from Falkirk Grahamston to the port of Grangemouth. The timetabled service actually operated between Larbert and Grangemouth, with Grahamston at its centre. This was an intense service with approximately 15 trains running in each direction on each weekday. There were additionally a handful of trains operating between Polmont and Larbert which crossed with the Larbert–Grangemouth services at Grahamston station. 'Dieselised' in the late 1950s using Gloucester two-car DMUs, the service was withdrawn in January 1968.

By 1960 various types of main-line diesel locomotive were working into and out of Glasgow's stations and depots. NBL/MAN Type 2s (Class 21) were working passenger trains from Queen Street to Fort William/Mallaig as well as from Buchanan Street to Stirling/Oban and to Perth/Dundee, while English Electric Type 4s (Class 40) were to be seen in greater numbers at Central station on named

expresses from London, and BR/Sulzer 'Peak' Type 4s (Class 45 or 46) were operating over the old 'Sou'West' route into St Enoch. As the 1960s progressed other main-line types appeared in the Glasgow area, large numbers of BRCW/Sulzer Type 2s (Class 27) being allocated to Eastfield depot and Clayton Type 1s (Class 17) to Polmadie. Several English Electric Type 3s (Class 37) were also allocated to Polmadie in 1966.

The 1960s witnessed massive changes in the Glasgow transport scene, the Corporation's tramway system closing in September 1962, but the underground railway, run-down and desperately in need of modernisation, would have to wait until the 1970s for this to be effected. The most famous of locomotive builders, the North British Locomotive Co, went into liquidation in the spring of 1962 and closed soon after. Two of the city's main-line stations — St Enoch and Buchanan Street — also closed, in 1966, services being transferred to Central and Queen Street stations respectively.

On the plus side, 1960 saw one of the most significant changes to the city's transport system — the 'Blue Train' services. Included within the BTC's Modernisation Plan had been a proposal for the electrification of 190 miles of Glasgow suburban lines. This proceeded so rapidly that the first service, between Queen Street Low Level, Airdrie and Helensburgh, began in November 1960, to be followed in May 1962 by services from Central to Motherwell and Neilston and the Cathcart Circle.

Saturday 10 April 1971

Clayton Type 1 No D8568 trundles past Polmadie depot with a Class 9 goods carrying steel pipes. Never renumbered in the TOPS scheme, this locomotive would be withdrawn in October 1971. The only member of the class to survive and pass into preservation, it is currently based on the Chinnor & Princes Risborough Railway. *N. E. Preedy*

Left:
Wednesday 21 July 1965
BR/Sulzer Type 2 No D5081 leaves Gourock with the 17.05 to Glasgow Central. This locomotive would be withdrawn in October 1980 as No 24 081 (the last of its class to survive in normal service), duly passing into preservation, and is currently based on the Gloucestershire–Warwickshire Railway. *A. D. McVean*

Top right:
Wednesday 25 May 1966
The up 'Mid-day Scot' leaves Glasgow Central behind Brush/Sulzer Type 4 No D1858. This locomotive would be withdrawn (as No 47 208) in January 1980 after an accident. *C. Lofthus*

Lower right:
Wednesday 30 October 1968
BRCW/Sulzer Type 2 No D5367 prepares to leave Glasgow Central with a train of empty carriage stock. Renumbered 27 021, it would be withdrawn in June 1985. *C. P. Boocock*

Tuesday 29 August 1961
BRCW/Sulzer Type 2 No D5348 climbs Cowlairs Incline with
the 3.50pm Glasgow Queen Street–Mallaig, assisted at the
rear by ex-LNER Class V3 2-6-2T No 67600. The 'V3' would be
withdrawn from service in December 1962, No D5348
(as 27 002) in January 1986. *William Russell*

Saturday 23 March 1963

A Swindon-built six-car 'Inter-City' DMU operating an Edinburgh Waverley–Glasgow Queen Street service near Cadder Yard.
The leading car is No Sc79107. *S. Rickard*

Monday 8 July 1963

A pair of Clayton Type 1s — Nos D8534 and D8537 — wait to leave Ravenscraig No 3 steel mill with a Class 4 goods train
of strip coil bound for Gartcosh. Both locomotives would be withdrawn in 1968, No D8537 in July
and No D8534 in October. *W. S. Sellar*

Saturday 20 May 1961
A Swindon-built six-car 'Inter-City' DMU arrives at Glasgow St Enoch as the 3.30pm service from Ayr. This was one of the second batch of 'Inter-City' units, introduced in 1959 for services between Glasgow and Ayr, Girvan, Stranraer, Largs and Ardrossan. Note the Caledonian-style route indicator still in use above the buffer. *S. Rickard*

Friday 12 June 1964
On a fill-in turn, LMR-allocated BR/Sulzer Type 2 No D5082 passes Thorntonhall station, on the East Kilbride branch, with a goods train for Glasgow. This locomotive would be withdrawn in March 1979 as No 24 082. *W. A. C. Smith*

Tuesday 11 August 1959
A Glasgow Central–East Kilbride service operated by three two-car Metro-Cammell DMUs passes the site of Clarkston East Junction.
G. H. Robin

Saturday 29 August 1964
A local train formed of a three-car Derby DMU and a two-car Gloucester unit leaves Ibrox station for Glasgow Central.
K. M. Andrew

Top left:
Saturday 4 July 1964
BR/Sulzer Type 2 No D5182 passes Robroyston West Junction with a Glasgow Buchanan Street–Oban passenger train. Renumbered 25 032, the locomotive would survive until March 1986. *S. Rickard*

Lower left:
Saturday 4 July 1964
Clayton Type 1 No D8533 passes Robroyston West Junction with a Class 6 goods. This locomotive would be withdrawn in October 1968. *S. Rickard*

Thursday 12 May 1960
Looking still to be in fine condition, having been delivered the previous October, BRCW/Sulzer Type 2 No D5344 awaits its next duty at St Rollox depot. In the background is ex-LMS Class 5MT 4-6-0 No 44978. The 'Black Five' would be withdrawn in July 1965, No D5344 (renumbered 26 044) in January 1984. *G. W. Morrison*

**Tuesday
26 November 1963**
NBL Type 2 No D6123 passes St Rollox with the 10.15am Glasgow Buchanan Street–Aberdeen. Earlier in the year this locomotive had been re-equipped with a Paxman engine in an attempt to improve its reliability, but it would nevertheless be withdrawn in September 1971. *Norman Pollock*

Top right:
Saturday 5 January 1963
English Electric Type 1 No D8080 skirts St Rollox depot, between Balornock and Germiston junctions, with a down goods. This locomotive would be withdrawn as No 20 080 in July 1990. *S. Rickard*

Lower right:
Saturday 5 January 1963
NBL/MAN Type 2 No D6102 approaches St Rollox depot at the head of the 1.15pm Glasgow Buchanan Street–Dundee. This locomotive would subsequently be rebuilt with a Paxman engine, prolonging its life until October 1971. *S. Rickard*

Friday 2 November 1962
The last 12.45pm Glasgow Buchanan Street–Gartcosh leaves St Rollox station behind NBL/MAN Type 2 No D6125. This locomotive would be withdrawn in December 1967. *S. Rickard*

Wednesday 10 July 1963
Re-equipped with a 1,350hp Paxman 'Ventura' engine in an attempt to improve reliability, NBL Type 2 No D6123 stands at Fullwood Junction in ex-works condition with a test train of 10 coaches. This locomotive was the first of its class to be re-engined; eventually 20 locomotives would be so treated. *W. S. Sellar*

Monday 15 June 1959
Arriving at Queen Street station, a two-car Metro-Cammell DMU emerges from the gloom of the tunnels and passes beneath the impressive signal gantry. The leading vehicle is No SC51250.
R. F. Roberts

Saturday 6 July 1963
BR/Sulzer 'Peak' Type 4 No D87 at the head of a southbound coal train on Cumbernauld Bank. This locomotive would be withdrawn as No 45 127 in May 1987. *Derek Cross*

Monday 30 March 1964
NBL/MAN Type 2 No D6104 pilots ex-LMS Class 5MT 4-6-0 No 44902 on an up express passing Greenhill. The driver of the 'Black Five' is taking time to acknowledge the signalman. No D6104 would be withdrawn in December 1967, outlasting No 44902 by just two months! *Paul Riley*

Tuesday 14 June 1966
BRCW/Sulzer Type 2 No D5310 near Cumbernauld at the head of the 11.15 Glasgow Buchanan Street–Dundee. Withdrawn in December 1992 as No 26 010, this locomotive would pass into preservation on the Northampton & Lamport Railway. *C. T. Gifford*

Saturday 13 May 1961
The 8.58am departure to Glasgow Central, formed of two three-car Derby lightweight DMUs, waits to leave Cathcart. The leading car is No SC51997. Several cars from this class have passed into preservation. *M. Mensing*

Saturday 8 August 1964
Seen heading a Class 9 goods train at Robroyston East Junction is Clayton Type 1 No D8523, which would survive in service only until October 1968. *S. Rickard*

Monday 24 July 1961

A Swindon-built 'Inter-City' DMU awaits departure from Largs as the 4.5pm to Glasgow St Enoch. *S. Rickard*

Saturday 15 June 1963

Forming the 12.45pm service from Glasgow St Enoch, a pair of two-car Gloucester DMUs leave Stevenston for Largs. *S. Rickard*

Saturday 3 October 1964
Working a service to Lanark, a two-car Gloucester DMU calls at the remote Inches station on the last day of operation on the Muirkirk branch. *David C. Smith*

Friday 22 May 1964
A two-car Metro-Cammell DMU leaves Inches station, on the Lanark–Muirkirk branch, bound for Muirkirk. The photograph shows clearly the remoteness of this location. *J. Spencer Gilks*

Tuesday 13 August 1963
A two-car Gloucester DMU leaves Muirkirk as the 12.41pm service to Lanark.
D. A. McNaught

Thursday 20 June 1963
A service from Grangemouth formed of a two-car Gloucester DMU passes Larbert South signalbox as it arrives at Larbert station.
S. Rickard

**Saturday
25 November 1961**
BRCW/Sulzer Type 2
No D5349 waits to leave
Grangemouth station with
the 12.4pm to Glasgow
Buchanan Street. This
locomotive would be
withdrawn in January 1987
as No 27 003. *W. A. C. Smith*

Friday 15 September 1961
English Electric Type 4
No D281 at the head of the
down 'North Briton' between
Polmont and Falkirk High.
This locomotive would be
withdrawn as No 40 081 in
February 1983. *S. Rickard*

**Tuesday
1 September 1964**
A two-car Gloucester DMU leaves Larbert as the 17.53 service to Grangemouth. The leading car is No SC51113.
R. Nelson

Thursday 20 June 1963
On a very wet day at Falkirk Grahamston station a two-car Gloucester DMU (left) waits to leave as the 10.55am to Grangemouth while a similar unit (right, with car SC51123 bringing up the rear) calls with the 10.38am service from Larbert to Polmont.
S. Rickard

The West

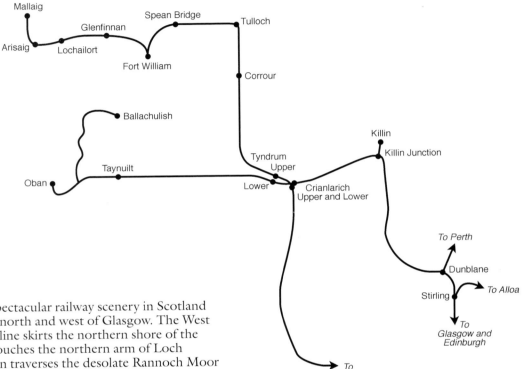

The most spectacular railway scenery in Scotland lies to the north and west of Glasgow. The West Highland line skirts the northern shore of the Firth of Clyde, touches the northern arm of Loch Lomond and then traverses the desolate Rannoch Moor before turning west at Tulloch and heading toward the rugged countryside surrounding Fort William and the extension to Mallaig. In 1960 steam power still reigned supreme, with ex-LMS 'Black Five' 4-6-0s and the ex-LNER 2-6-0s operating most of the services. In 1961 diesel locomotives, in the shape of NBL/MAN Type 2s (Class 21) and BRCW/Sulzer Type 2s (Class 27) were to be seen working alongside them; by 1962 the steam locomotives had gone, but the line's passenger and goods traffic remained in the hands of the NBL and BRCW diesels until the late 1960s, when withdrawals of the former began.

The second line that made its way into this impressive part of Scotland was that heading north and west from Stirling to Oban. Striking off the main line at Dunblane and running through the splendid countryside toward Callander and Killin Junction, it then turned sharply west to Crianlarich, where it crossed the West Highland line. Unfortunately, this section of the line was closed abruptly in September 1965 after a severe landslide affected the track near Glenoglehead. This led to Oban trains' having to use the West Highland line from Glasgow to Crianlarich, where they diverted onto the original route. From Crianlarich the line passes through Glen Lochy and the rugged Pass of Brander before reaching Oban. This line saw mainly steam traction (mostly ex-LMS and Standard Class 5 4-6-0s) until 1961, whereafter duties were shared with NBL/MAN and BRCW/Sulzer Type 2 diesels. By 1962 the steam locomotives had been banished, the two diesel types continuing to work all traffic until the NBL locomotives started to be withdrawn in the late 1960s.

Saturday 1 June 1963
Returning from Mallaig with the 'Jacobite' special between Lochailort and Glenfinnan is BRCW/Sulzer Type 2 No D5351. Note the number of wooden-bodied Gresley coaches in the consist. Withdrawn (as No 27 005) in July 1987, the locomotive is now preserved by the SRPS at Bo'ness. *G. W. Morrison*

Friday 13 July 1962
Shunting in the yard at Fort William is BR/English Electric 0-6-0 No D4097. Renumbered 08 883, this locomotive is now owned by EWS. *Author*

Tuesday 7 May 1968
NBL Type 2 No D6107 leaves
Corrour station with the
06.00 Glasgow–Mallaig.
This locomotive would be
withdrawn in October 1971.
C. W. R. Bowman

Wednesday 15 July 1964
This stunning photograph shows BRCW/Sulzer Type 2
No D5366 crossing Glenfinnan Viaduct with a Fort
William–Mallaig passenger train. The locomotive
would be withdrawn from service in April 1986
as No 27 020. *Paul Riley*

Friday 13 July 1962
A crew member of BRCW /
Sulzer Type 2 No D5356
prepares to hand over the
single-line token as he
approaches Fort William
station. This station, which
stood in the town centre, on
the shore of Loch Linnhe,
would close in June 1975 to
make way for a town by-pass,
a new station a short distance
from the original being opened
at the same time. *Author*

Top right:
Saturday 24 August 1968
NBL/Paxman Type 2 No D6133 approaches Arisaig with
the 17.35 Mallaig–Fort William. The locomotive would be
withdrawn in December 1971. *C. Lofthus*

Lower right:
Thursday 27 May 1965
Nearing the end of its journey, BRCW/Sulzer Type 2 No D5349
approaches Fort William with the 19.30 King's Cross–Fort William
sleeper. This locomotive would be withdrawn as No 27 003
in January 1987. *Noel A. Machell*

Friday 15 August 1969
BRCW/Sulzer Type 2
No D5415 waits to leave
Mallaig with the 14.05 to
Fort William. This locomotive
would be withdrawn from
service in July 1980 as
No 27 044. *N. E. Preedy*

Thursday 9 April 1964
Running into Spean Bridge
station with the 09.40
Fort William–Glasgow is
BRCW/Sulzer Type 2
No D5350. Renumbered
27 004, this locomotive
would be withdrawn in May
1986. *Anthony A. Vickers*

Saturday 20 April 1968
Dominated by McCaig's tower, NBL/Paxman Type 2 No D6101 leaves Oban station with a service for Glasgow.
The locomotive would be withdrawn in August 1971. *Derek Cross*

Friday 3 April 1964
BRCW/Sulzer Type 2 No D5364 prepares to leave Ballachulish (Glencoe) station with the 16.10 to Oban.
This branch would close to all traffic from 28 March 1966, but the locomotive would survive (latterly as No 27 018)
for a further 20 years, until May 1986. *Ian G. Holt*

Saturday 10 August 1963
BRCW/Sulzer Type 2
No D5357 (left) prepares
to leave Oban station with
the 12.5pm to Glasgow
Buchanan Street as sister
locomotive No D5358 (right)
shunts empty coaching stock.
No D5357 would be
withdrawn (as 27 011) in
March 1981, No D5358
following (as 27 012)
in May 1986. *J. D. Benson*

Tuesday 17 May 1960
Introduced in 1959,
a Swindon-built three-car
'Cross-Country' DMU
approaches Taynuilt station
with a Glasgow Queen Street–
Oban excursion. The leading
car is No Sc51794.
M. Mensing

Above:

Wednesday 25 August 1965

Waiting to leave Oban station with the 12.20 to Glasgow Buchanan Street is BRCW/Sulzer Type 2 No D5359. The observation car (left) has arrived on the rear of the 07.55 from Buchanan Street. Renumbered 27 013, No D5359 would be withdrawn in July 1976. *Stephen Tallis*

Left:

Wednesday 28 April 1971

This moody photograph, with Ben More towering in the background, shows BRCW/Sulzer Type 2 No D5358 hurrying the 08.35 Glasgow–Oban between Crianlarich and Tyndrum Lower. *J. H. Cooper-Smith*

Right:

Wednesday 2 September 1964

NBL Type 2 No D6129 waits at Tyndrum Lower station as BRCW/Sulzer Type 2 No D5357 approaches with a goods train from Oban. No D6129 would be withdrawn in October 1971, nearly a decade before No D5357. *John R. Hillier*

The West Coast Main Line

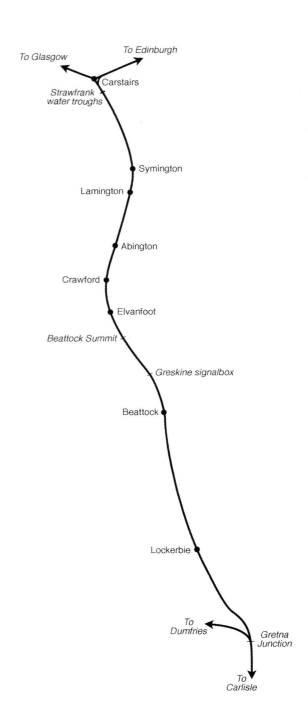

To Glasgow

To Edinburgh

Carstairs

Strawfrank water troughs

Symington

Lamington

Abington

Crawford

Elvanfoot

Beattock Summit

Greskine signalbox

Beattock

Lockerbie

To Dumfries

Gretna Junction

To Carlisle

By the summer of 1959 English Electric Type 4 (Class 40) locomotives were being delivered to the London Midland Region, and it was not long before they started to replace steam on the named expresses running between London and Glasgow. Trains such as the 'Royal Scot', 'Mid-Day Scot' and 'Caledonian', once hauled by powerful Stanier-designed 'Coronation' Pacifics, were now being handled by this new generation of locomotives. In the mid-1960s the route still saw many steam workings, especially during the traditional Glasgow Fair holiday fortnight during the latter half of July, when many special trains were run from Glasgow to the Lancashire coast and to North Wales. However, diesel traction was quickly replacing steam on the old Caledonian Railway route north of Carlisle, English Electric Type 4s becoming more numerous on passenger workings and being joined by increasing numbers of Brush/Sulzer Type 4s (Class 47). Other types of diesel locomotives to be seen working over this route during the 1960s were BR/Sulzer Type 2s (Class 25) on passenger trains and English Electric Type 1s (Class 20) and Clayton Type 1s (Class 17) working goods traffic.

Early in 1965 the majority of the intermediate stations between Carstairs and Carlisle were closed; Thankerton, Symington, Lamington, Abington, Crawford and Elvanfoot all lost their passenger services and eventually had their platforms removed in preparation for the work on the extension of West Coast electrification to Glasgow. During 1967/8 the later English Electric Type 4s (Class 50) were introduced specifically to haul the Anglo-Scottish traffic north of Crewe, and these locomotives could be seen, either singly or in pairs, hauling both passenger and goods traffic over this route until the early 1970s, when they were gradually displaced by the aforementioned extension of the West Coast electrification.

**Saturday
15 August 1970**
BR/Sulzer Type 2 No D7591
heads north from Carstairs
with some empty coaching
stock. The locomotive would
be withdrawn as No 25 241
in May 1981. *Derek Cross*

Saturday 13 July 1963
Clayton Type 1 No D8510
trundles through Carstairs
with a goods train heading
for Glasgow. The locomotive
would be withdrawn in
March 1971. *Author*

Thursday 30 May 1963

English Electric Type 4 No D338 passes Braidwood signalbox with a Glasgow–Plymouth service. This locomotive would be withdrawn from service as No 40 138 in August 1982. *Derek Cross*

Saturday 15 August 1970

No D433, one of the later design of English Electric Type 4s introduced in 1967, approaches Carstairs with a train from Perth. Later renumbered 50 033 and named *Glorious*, this locomotive would be withdrawn from service in 1994. Following a spell as part of the National Collection at York, it is now a static exhibit at the Steam Museum at Swindon. *Derek Cross*

Saturday 8 April 1961
The up 'Royal Scot' speeds through Lamington with English Electric Type 4 No D301 in charge. Latterly numbered 40 101, this locomotive be withdrawn in August 1982. *Derek Cross*

Wednesday 10 July 1968
Having come to the rescue of failed English Electric Type 4 No D401, Brush/Sulzer Type 4 No D1848 heads the 11.30 Birmingham–Glasgow Central past Symington. No D1848 would be withdrawn in April 1989 as No 47 198, while No D401 would become No 50 001 *Dreadnought*, remaining in service as such until April 1991. *I. Strachan*

Top left:

Saturday 8 June 1963

English Electric Type 4 No D335 crosses the River Clyde just south of Carstairs at the head of a Perth–London express. Renumbered 40 135 under TOPS, following withdrawal from normal service in 1985 the locomotive passed into Departmental stock as No 97 406, being finally withdrawn in December 1986. Now preserved, it is currently based on the East Lancashire Railway. *Derek Cross*

Lower left:

Saturday 15 August 1970

A pair of BR/Sulzer Type 2s, No D7634 leading No D7671, seen near Lamington with a Blackpool–Glasgow relief. No D7634 would be withdrawn as No 25 284 in January 1985, whilst No D7671 would survive (as No 25 321) until September 1986, passing thereafter into preservation at the Midland Railway Centre, Butterley. *Derek Cross*

Saturday 6 June 1970

Bereft of its *Andania* nameplates, English Electric Type 4 No D213 is seen at the head of a soda-ash train between Lamington and Abington. Withdrawn (as No 40 013) in January 1985 and bought privately for preservation, this locomotive is currently undergoing restoration at the Barrow Hill Roundhouse. *J. H. Cooper-Smith*

Friday 5 June 1970
A pair of the later English
Electric Type 4s — Nos D437
and D402 — seen between
Abington and Crawford at the
head of the 16.00 Glasgow–
Euston. Both locomotives
would be withdrawn in
September 1991, as No 50 037
Illustrious and No 50 002
Superb respectively; the
latter is still extant and is
currently awaiting repair at
the Barrow Hill Roundhouse.
J. H. Cooper-Smith

Top right:
Tuesday 31 March 1964
The up 'Royal Scot', hauled by English Electric Type 4 No D226,
being diverted through the loop at Elvanfoot station.
The locomotive would be withdrawn from service in April
1980 as No 40 026. *Derek Cross*

Lower right:
Saturday 1 August 1970
Brush/Sulzer Type 4 No D1850 (later numbered 47 200)
hurrying south near Elvanfoot with the Perth–London
(Kensington) car-carrier service. At the time of writing the
locomotive remains active with Cotswold Rail Engineering.
Derek Cross

Top left:

Monday 24 April 1961

The down 'Royal Scot' passes Beattock Summit signalbox behind English Electric Type 4 No D299. The photographer noted that this appeared to be a regular turn for a diesel so long as the load did not exceed eight coaches, heavier loads generally producing a steam locomotive. Latterly numbered 40 099, No D299 would be withdrawn in October 1984. *Derek Cross*

Lower left:

Saturday 21 June 1969

English Electric Type 4 No D443 powers the 08.35 Birmingham–Perth around the sweeping curve past the site of Elvanfoot station. This locomotive would be withdrawn in February 1991 as No 50 043 *Eagle*. *P. W. Robinson*

Saturday 25 August 1962

Another photograph of the down 'Royal Scot' passing Beattock Summit, this time with '12 on'. The train engine, English Electric Type 4 No D308, appears to be struggling with the load and is being assisted at the rear by *two* bankers. Built by Robert Stephenson & Hawthorn Ltd, it would be withdrawn in August 1980 as No 40 108. *Derek Cross*

Sunday 15 October 1967
Brush/Sulzer Type 4
No D1844 (later 47 194)
nearing Beattock Summit
with a Birmingham–Glasgow
passenger train. Note the
wrong-line working. Last
used in July 1999, the
locomotive is currently in
store in the ownership of
Direct Rail Services.
C. Lofthus

Top right:
Monday 15 April 1963
English Electric Type 4 No D325 passes Greskine signalbox
on the climb to Beattock Summit with the down 'Royal Scot'.
This locomotive would be withdrawn in June 1981 as
No 40 125. *J. S. Whiteley*

Lower right:
Monday 29 May 1967
Brush/Sulzer Type 4 No D1632 between Hartshope and
Beattock Summit at the head of a Birmingham–Glasgow
express. The locomotive would be withdrawn in November
1994 as No 47 050. *John M. Boyes*

Left:
Saturday 21 June 1969
English Electric Type 4
No D435 accelerates away
from Beattock station
with the 11.35 Birmingham–
Glasgow. This locomotive
would remain in service until
August 1990, latterly as
No 50 035 *Ark Royal*; now
preserved, it is currently
based on the Severn Valley
Railway. *P. W. Robinson*

Top right:
Saturday 8 August 1964
An odd pairing of diesel
traction near Gretna Junction,
English Electric Type 1
No D8115 piloting English
Electric Type 4 No D313
on a Glasgow–Birmingham
express. Latterly numbered
40 113, No D313 would be
withdrawn in October 1981,
No D8115 surviving until
January 1987 as 20 115.
Derek Cross

Lower right:
Saturday 15 July 1967
Brush/Sulzer Type 4
No D1808 enters Beattock
station with a southbound
Freightliner. The station was
to close early in 1972;
the locomotive would
survive (latterly as
No 47 327) until February
1993. *Ian Allan Library*

Ayrshire and the South West

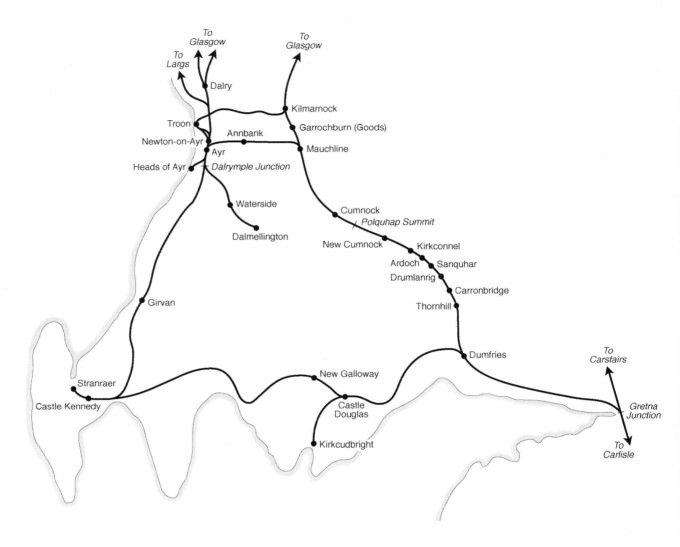

To Glasgow

To Glasgow

To Largs

Dalry

Kilmarnock

Troon

Annbank

Garrochburn (Goods)

Newton-on-Ayr

Mauchline

Ayr

Heads of Ayr — Dalrymple Junction

Waterside

Cumnock

Polquhap Summit

Dalmellington

New Cumnock

Kirkconnel

Ardoch

Sanquhar

Drumlanrig

Carronbridge

Girvan

Thornhill

Dumfries

To Carstairs

New Galloway

Gretna Junction

Stranraer

Castle Kennedy

Castle Douglas

Kirkcudbright

To Carlisle

Railways in Ayrshire fell into two distinct groups — those serving the coastal holiday resorts, commuter towns and ferry services of the Firth of Clyde and those serving the extensive coal-mining area inland to the east and southeast of Ayr. The former, with services from Glasgow St Enoch to Largs, Ardrossan, Saltcoats, Troon, Prestwick, Ayr and Girvan were, from August 1959, operated by Swindon-built three- or six-car sets of 'Inter-City' DMUs (later Class 126), which units continued to operate the service until withdrawal in the early 1980s.

During the 1960s coal traffic in Ayrshire consisted mainly of exports to Northern Ireland shipped from Ayr harbour and deliveries to the coal-fired power stations in the Glasgow area. Motive power for these intensive workings was steam, mostly in the form of ex-LMS 'Crab' 2-6-0s and vintage ex-CR 0-6-0s. By the mid-1960s other classes were being transferred from depots on the east coast, and ex-LMS 'Black Five' and even ex-LNER 'B1' 4-6-0s were tried on this traffic. Some Standard Class 4 2-6-0s were also to be seen working these coal trains. The inevitable occurred in October 1966, when the remaining

Saturday 19 August 1967
BR/Sulzer Type 4 No D26 passes through Kilmarnock with the 16.05 Glasgow Central–Leeds.
This locomotive would be withdrawn from service as No 45 020 in December 1985. *C. Lofthus*

steam traction in Ayrshire was withdrawn and diesel power took over. Several types — English Electric Type 1s (Class 20), BRCW/Sulzer Type 2s (Class 27), BR/Sulzer Type 2s (Class 25) and even the short-lived Clayton Type 1s (Class 17) — could be seen working the coal traffic, often singly but usually in pairs on the heavier trains.

From 1960 passenger traffic on the 'Sou'West' main line from Glasgow St Enoch to Dumfries, Carlisle, Leeds and the South was rapidly turned over to diesel power in the form of BR/Sulzer 'Peak' Type 4s (Classes 45 and 46), which became the prime motive power for the through trains on this route, BRCW/Sulzer Type 2s generally being seen on stopping trains. Although goods trains still saw the occasional steam working until the autumn of 1966, diesel locomotives such as Clayton and English Electric Type 1s and BR/Sulzer and BRCW/Sulzer Type 2s could also be seen working all types of goods trains on this route, including the heavy coal trains from Fauldhead Colliery (near Kirkconnel) to Ayr harbour.

To the south of Ayrshire and the west of Dumfries-shire, Kirkcudbright and Wigton were served by the 'Port Road', which meandered through busy market towns, such as Castle Douglas and Newton Stewart, and the sparsely populated inland villages of New Galloway and Gatehouse of Fleet, where the station was situated approximately six miles from the village. This was the shortest route for passenger trains from England to Stranraer to meet the ferries that sailed to Northern Ireland, and until the closure of the line in June 1965 Stranraer harbour was still served by three through trains from London Euston every weekday. Steam power handled nearly all the traffic on this line until closure, diesels making few appearances. After the closure of the 'Port Road' Stranraer kept its link with Glasgow St Enoch via Girvan, the service being operated by the Swindon-built 'Inter-City' DMUs which had been introduced to the route in 1959.

**Wednesday
2 October 1963**
Displaying a 65A (Eastfield)
shed code, NBL Type 2
No D6123 passes
Garrochburn signalbox at the
head of a test train including
a dynamometer car. The first
of its class to be re-equipped
with a Paxman engine in an
attempt to improve reliability,
the locomotive would remain
in service until September
1971. *Derek Cross*

July 1964
Garrochburn again, but this
time with a southbound
Class 4 goods train with
BRCW/Sulzer Type 2
No D5388 in charge. Initially
renumbered 27 105, this
locomotive would be
withdrawn in April 1987
as No 27 049. *Derek Cross*

August 1962
The down 'Thames–Clyde Express' passing Garrochburn behind BR/Sulzer Type 4 No D105.
This locomotive would be withdrawn in January 1985 as No 45 064. *Derek Cross*

Saturday 3 December 1966
BR/Sulzer Type 2 No D5132 passes Mauchline No 1 signalbox with a down soda-ash train.
The locomotive would be withdrawn as No 24 132 in February 1976. *C. Lofthus*

Saturday 14 April 1962
Photographed just north of Polquhap Summit, BR/Sulzer Type 4 No D16 heads for Glasgow with the overnight express from London St Pancras. Renumbered 45 016, this locomotive would be withdrawn in November 1985. *Derek Cross*

Friday 3 April 1964
A pair of Clayton Type 1s, Nos D8542 leading D8509, working a northbound Class 6 goods near New Cumnock. No D8509 would be withdrawn in October 1968, No D8542 following in October 1971. *Derek Cross*

Thursday 11 April 1968
BRCW/Sulzer Type 2
No D5354 leaves Kirkconnel
station with the two-coach
10.25 Leeds–Glasgow Central
stopping train.
The locomotive would be
withdrawn as No 27 008
in August 1987.
John M. Boyes

Thursday 11 April 1968
BR/Sulzer Type 2 No D7534
leaves Fauldhead Colliery,
near Kirkconnel, with a Class 8
coal train for Ayr harbour.
This locomotive would be
withdrawn in August 1983
as No 25 184. *John M. Boyes*

Friday 28 April 1967
BR/Sulzer Type 4 No D162 passes through Drumlanrig Gorge with a Luton–Glasgow car train. This locomotive would be withdrawn in November 1984 as No 46 025. *Derek Cross*

Saturday 14 July 1962
BR/Sulzer Type 4 No D144 eases through the Ardoch curves with the up 'Thames–Clyde Express'. Renumbered 46 007, this locomotive would be withdrawn in February 1982. *D. A. McNaught*

Saturday 4 July 1964
BR/Sulzer Type 4 No D15 near Carronbridge with a Leeds–Glasgow express.
The locomotive would be withdrawn as No 45 018 in January 1981. *Derek Cross*

Sunday 14 July 1963
Its 17A shed-code plate denoting allocation to Derby, BR/Sulzer Type 4 No D113 pauses at a very wet Dumfries with the up
'Thames-Clyde Express'. Latterly numbered 45 128, the locomotive would remain in service until August 1988. *M. Mensing*

Monday 12 August 1968
The 'Port Road' between Dumfries and Stranraer closed in June 1965, but the track was left *in situ* for several years before lifting commenced. Seen working a demolition train at New Galloway is BRCW/Sulzer Type 2 No D5407. Initially renumbered 27 114, this locomotive would be withdrawn in February 1986 as No 27 208. *Derek Cross*

Top right:
Friday 12 July 1963
A Swindon-built 'Inter-City' six-car DMU working the 9.0am Glasgow St Enoch–Stranraer service, seen approaching Castle Kennedy. *M. Mensing*

Lower right:
April 1969
At Waterside, on the Dalmellington branch, English Electric Type 1 No D8121 pilots BRCW/Sulzer Type 2 No D5404 on a Waterside–Ayr Harbour coal train. Here sporting a painted 66A (Polmadie) shed code on its buffer-beam, No D8121 (latterly 20 121) would be sold to DRS in July 1997. Initially renumbered 27 113 and later 27 207, No D5404 would be withdrawn from normal service in May 1986, passing into Departmental stock (as ADB 968025) before final withdrawal in July 1987. *Derek Cross*

Saturday 5 July 1969
Passing Ayr shed, another Swindon-built six-car 'Inter-City' DMU approaches Newton-on-Ayr on the 14.10 Ayr–Glasgow service. *Geoffrey J. Jackson*

Top right:
Saturday 5 July 1969
The 13.00 Glasgow–Ayr service passes Newton-on-Ayr, operated by yet another Swindon-built six-car 'Inter-City' DMU. *Geoffrey J. Jackson*

Lower right:
Monday 30 March 1959
Undergoing trials a week before entering service on the Dalmellington branch, Park Royal-built railbus No SC79974 is seen entering Ayr station. Sadly the experiment with railbuses did not save the branch, which would close to passenger traffic in April 1964, but this example would survive until November 1966. *G. H. Robin*

Monday 15 July 1963

Seen just short of their destination at Ayr station, Clayton Type 1s Nos D8538 and D8522 cross the River Ayr at the head of an excursion train from Law Junction. Lacking any steam-heating equipment, the Claytons were rarely seen on passenger workings. No D8522 would be withdrawn in October 1968, No D8538 lasting for a further three years, until October 1971.
Derek Cross

Wednesday 12 May 1965

Seen approaching Ayr with a goods train from Polmadie in Glasgow is BR/Sulzer Type 2 No D5133.
This locomotive would be withdrawn as No 24 133 in March 1978. *A. M. Bisset*

Monday 25 May 1964

Passing over the River Ayr on the approach to Ayr station is BR/Sulzer Type 4 No D19 with a Glasgow–Ayr relief. Allocated to Leeds Holbeck (55A) at the time of this photograph, the locomotive would be withdrawn in May 1981 as No 45 025. *Derek Cross*

Tuesday 20 June 1961

Operating the 12.55pm Stranraer Town–Glasgow St Enoch service, a Swindon-built 'Inter-City' DMU arrives at Ayr station. Apparent from this photograph is the very small driver's compartment of the Driving Motor Second Intermediate (leading), as, once again, is the continued use of the Caledonian-style route indicator above the buffer. *S. Rickard*

Index of Photographic Locations